AF367475

DIVERSITY IN VERTEBRATE LOCOMOTION

Diversity in Vertebrate Locomotion

From Fins to Wings

RAYAN MUSK

Mohammed Altaf Hussain

Contents

INDEX

INTRODUCTION

The ensemble of vertebrate life unfurls across an immense material of biological specialties, every species exceptionally adjusted to explore its current circumstance. Headway, the capacity to move starting with one spot then onto the next, lies at the core of vertebrate science, displaying a phenomenal cluster of transformations that have developed more than large number of years. From the smooth undulations of fish balances pushing through water to the lofty take off of birds through the skies, the variety in vertebrate motion is a demonstration of the transformative creativity that has impacted life on The planet.

This investigation leaves on a complete excursion through the domains of vertebrate motion, digging into the complexities of how various species have developed and calibrated their methods of development. The range of locomotor transformations traverses sea-going, earthbound, and ethereal areas, each introducing its own arrangement of difficulties and open doors. From the early oceanic trailblazers with crude blades to the avian marvels that oppose gravity with wings, the tale of vertebrate headway is a charming story of development, proficiency, and endurance.

1. Transformative Beginnings: From Antiquated Oceans to Different Territories
1. **Fish: Blades and the Introduction of Sea-going Motion**
   The starting points of vertebrate headway can be followed back to the old oceans where the main fish, furnished with crude blades, left on an excursion that would shape the eventual fate of vertebrate life. The development of balances denoted a crucial second in the progress from uninvolved floating to dynamic swimming, permitting fish to explore through water with momentous effectiveness. From the smoothed out groups of sharks to the complex blade designs of

beam finned fish, the sea-going world turned into a material for the development of different locomotor variations.

2. Creatures of land and water: The Trailblazers of Earthly Investigation

As vertebrates wandered past the watery domains, the rise of creatures of land and water denoted a vital developmental change. Outfitted with appendages, creatures of land and water explored both sea-going and earthly conditions, displaying the adaptability of appendage based movement. The difficulties of changing among water and land laid the preparation for ensuing transformations in tetrapods, making way for the triumph of new natural specialties.

II. Variety in Balance Designs: The Oceanic Orchestra

1. Fish Blades: From Stabilizers to Propellers
The balance designs of fish are a demonstration of the variety of oceanic movement methodologies. While certain blades act as stabilizers, keeping up with equilibrium and mobility, others capability as propellers, impelling fish through water with noteworthy accuracy. The advancement of dorsal, pectoral, pelvic, and butt-centric balances features the adaptability of blade variations across various species, each finely tuned to the particular requests of their sea-going natural surroundings.

2. Beam Finned Fish: Accuracy and Mobility

Among the horde types of fish balances, the beam finned assortment stands apart for its unpredictable plan and various capabilities. Beam finned fish, including most of fish species, show an extensive variety of balance morphologies adjusted for accuracy, mobility, and speed. The advancement of specific balances, for example, the extended pectoral blades of flying fish, features the astounding manners by which balances have been adjusted to take advantage of biological specialties and dodge hunters.

III. Systems of Drive in Fish: Unwinding the Submerged Expressive dance

1. Undulating Bodies and Caudal Blades
The entrancing undulations of fish bodies, combined with the propulsive power created by caudal blades, structure the groundwork of submerged motion. The variety in caudal balance shapes, from forked tails for speed to lunate tails for perseverance, mirrors the

versatile reactions of fish to their environmental prerequisites. The intricate interchange between body developments and blade capability makes a submerged expressive dance that differs across species, each arranged for explicit environments and ways of life.

2. Fly Drive and Hydrodynamics

Past undulatory motion, some fish have developed cunning components for drive. Stream drive, exemplified by squids and certain fish species, includes ousting water quickly to create forward movement. The hydrodynamics of fly drive exhibit the union of structure and capability, empowering fish to explore through water with accuracy and speed. Understanding these systems gives experiences into the developmental advancements that have formed the hydrodynamic productivity of fish headway.

IV. Developmental Changes in Fish Headway: Exploring Dynamic Conditions

1. From Water to Land: The Jump of Tetrapods
The change from water to land denoted a significant second in vertebrate development, with tetrapods (four-limbed vertebrates) driving the way.
The appendages that at first advanced for help and development in oceanic conditions became fundamental apparatuses for exploring earthly scenes. The difficulties of rising up out of water to colonize new living spaces drove the development of different appendage structures, making way for the earthbound motion of creatures of land and water, reptiles, birds, and vertebrates.
2. Fish that Walk and Inhale Air

Shockingly, some fish species have additionally embraced earthbound life, showing the adaptability of locomotor variations. Fish like the mudskipper have changed pectoral blades that capability as appendages, permitting them to "stroll" ashore. Furthermore, transformations for air-breathing, for example, maze organs in specific fish, grandstand the developmental pliancy that empowers these amphibian animals to take advantage of both water and land conditions.

V. Creatures of land and water: The Developmental Progress Bosses

1. From Water-Subordinate Hatchlings to Earthly Grown-ups
Creatures of land and water, with their exceptional life cycle incorporating sea-going hatchlings and earthbound grown-ups, represent

the transformative progress from water to land. Appendages that developed for help in water became instrumental for earthbound velocity. The difficulties of exploring different conditions prompted the development of particular variations, like the strong rear appendages of frogs for jumping and the tunneling abilities of lizards. Creatures of land and water, as trailblazers of earthbound investigation, established the groundwork for resulting tetrapod variety.

2. Appendage Variety and Versatile Radiation

The variety of appendage structures among creatures of land and water exhibits the versatile radiation that happened as these vertebrates expanded to take advantage of different biological specialties. From the lengthened digits of tree frogs for moving to the powerful appendages of tunneling lizards, creatures of land and water have developed a variety of appendage morphologies customized to their particular locomotor requirements. Understanding the appendage transformations of creatures of land and water gives bits of knowledge into the developmental cycles that energized their progress in assorted earthly natural surroundings.

VI. Requirements and Difficulties in Land and water proficient Motion: The Cost of Adaptability

1. Enthusiastic Expenses of Land and/or water capable Ways of life
While the change from water to land presented new open doors, it likewise achieved difficulties and requirements. Creatures of land and water, with their land and/or water capable ways of life, face vigorous expenses related with keeping up with physiological transformations for both amphibian and earthbound conditions. The need to explore assorted environments comes at the cost of expanded energy consumption, affecting taking care of ways of behaving, regenerative methodologies, and in general life history characteristics.

2. Natural surroundings Misfortune and Sickness Dangers

Land and water proficient populaces, previously wrestling with the lively requests of their land and/or water capable ways of life, face extra dangers from territory misfortune and sicknesses, for example, chytridiomycosis. Natural surroundings obliteration upsets the fragile harmony between oceanic reproducing destinations and earthbound searching grounds, while arising sicknesses present serious dangers to land and water proficient populaces around the world. Protection endeavors should address these difficulties to guarantee the proceeded with endurance of creatures of land and water and their novel locomotor transformations.

In the multifaceted embroidered artwork of vertebrate movement, the advances from blades to appendages and from water to land address great achievements in transformative history. The story unfurls across different living spaces, every variation finely tuned to the requests of explicit conditions. From the undulating developments of fish blades in oceanic domains to the perplexing appendage designs of creatures of land and water exploring earthbound scenes, the transformative advancements in vertebrate motion feature the striking variety that emerges from the exchange of structure, capability, and environmental difficulties.

In the resulting segments of this investigation, we will travel through the domains of reptiles, birds, and warm blooded animals, each contributing its part to the amazing story of vertebrate motion. The variety in locomotor transformations across these vertebrate gatherings uncovers the complicated arrangements that have arisen in light of the difficulties presented by different living spaces, natural specialties, and methods of life. As we dig into the developmental complexities of each gathering, the general account of locomotor variety will unfurl, outlining the entrancing excursion from blades to wings in the great embroidered artwork of vertebrate life.

1. Brief Overview of Vertebrate Locomotion

Vertebrate motion is a dynamic and different field that envelops the different manners by which creatures travel through their surroundings. From the liquid undulations of fish balances in sea-going domains to the taking off trips of birds through the skies, vertebrates have advanced a noteworthy cluster of locomotor transformations. This outline investigates the major standards and key qualities of vertebrate velocity, giving an expansive viewpoint on how various gatherings of vertebrates have dominated development to make due, duplicate, and flourish in their particular environments.

1. Groundworks of Vertebrate Velocity
1. Transformative Beginnings and Versatile Radiation
   The foundations of vertebrate velocity follow back to old sea-going conditions, where the initial fish advanced blades for impetus through water. This transformative advancement set up for the versatile radiation of vertebrates, prompting the development of assorted locomotor systems across various environments. From the water-to-land change of tetrapods to the specific variations of

ethereal fliers, the primary standards of vertebrate velocity lie in the developmental history of these noteworthy creatures.

2. The Job of Appendages: Tetrapod Changes

The development of appendages denoted a huge achievement in vertebrate headway, empowering tetrapods to investigate earthbound conditions. Appendages, whether adjusted for strolling, running, climbing, or flying, feature the flexibility of vertebrate development. The variety in appendage structures among tetrapods, from the strong appendages of warm blooded animals to the wings of birds, mirrors the variations expected to explore the difficulties presented by various environmental specialties.

II. Amphibian Motion: Blades, Tails, and Smoothed out Plans

1. Fish Motion: Undulations and Balances
   Fish, as trailblazers of vertebrate motion, display a large number of variations for proficient development in sea-going conditions. Undulatory developments of the body, fueled by particular muscles, push fish through water. The variety in balance structures, including dorsal, pectoral, pelvic, and butt-centric blades, adds to strength, mobility, and speed. The multifaceted interchange between body undulations and balance developments makes an orchestra of oceanic motion techniques.

2. Smoothed out Plans and Hydrodynamics

The smoothed out body states of fish are finely tuned for hydrodynamic effectiveness, lessening drag and empowering quick developments.

From the fusiform collections of quick swimming hunters to the straightened states of base dwelling species, the variety in body plans mirrors the natural specialties involved by various fish. Hydrodynamics, the investigation of smooth movement, assumes a critical part in understanding how fish explore through water with negligible opposition.

III. Earthly Motion: Appendages, Strides, and Concentrated Variations

1. Tetrapod Earthbound Headway
   The progress from water to land in tetrapods delivered a horde of earthly movement methodologies. Appendages, at first developed for help and development in amphibian conditions, became fundamental apparatuses for exploring assorted scenes. The advancement of various steps, including strolling, running, bouncing, and creeping,

exhibits the versatile adaptability of tetrapod headway. The advancement of appendage structures, joint explanations, and solid plans mirrors the particular requests of earthbound conditions.

2. Cursorial Variations: Speed and Dexterity

A few earthly vertebrates have developed cursorial variations for fast development. Cheetahs, for instance, have specific appendage muscles and a lightweight form, permitting them to accomplish exceptional rates in quest for prey. Variations for cursorial motion stretch out past well evolved creatures to incorporate birds and, surprisingly, certain reptiles. The concurrent development of cursorial highlights underscores the particular tensions leaning toward speed and readiness in unambiguous environmental settings.

IV. Aeronautical Velocity: Wings, Plumes, and Dominance of the Skies

1. Avian Flight: The Victory of Plumes and Wings
The development of trip in birds addresses a zenith of vertebrate headway. Padded wings, lightweight skeletons, and strong flight muscles empower birds to challenge gravity and navigate the skies with accuracy. The intricacies of avian flight stretch out to specific ways of behaving, for example, floating, taking off, and perplexing airborne moves. The variety in wing morphologies, from the taking off wings of falcons to the fast beats of hummingbird wings, grandstands the versatility of birds to differed biological specialties.

2. Bats: Mammalian Trailblazers of Flight

Bats, the main warm blooded creatures fit for supported flight, have developed special variations for airborne motion. Adaptable wings framed by lengthened fingers, fueled flight muscles, and echolocation capacities add to their authority of the nighttime skies. The intermingling of bat and bird flight represents the assorted transformative pathways prompting the procurement of trip inside various vertebrate gatherings.

V. Shared Standards and Merged Development

1. Biomechanical Standards of Headway
In spite of the variety in locomotor variations, certain biomechanical standards underlie vertebrate development. The organized activity of muscles, the job of skeletal designs, and the standards of energy effectiveness add to the outcome of various locomotor procedures. Understanding these common standards gives bits of knowledge

into the joined development of comparative locomotor transformations across remotely related vertebrate gatherings.

2. Merged Development in Locomotor Transformations

Merged development is a repetitive topic in vertebrate movement,
where comparable variations advance freely in various heredities. Models
incorporate smoothed out body structures in dolphins and ichthyosaurs
for productive oceanic motion, or cursorial variations in cheetahs and
ostriches for fast earthly development. Joined advancement features the
job of environmental tensions in molding versatile answers for normal
difficulties.

VI. Difficulties and Requirements in Vertebrate Movement

1. Enthusiastic Expenses and Compromises
   The effectiveness of vertebrate movement accompanies related
   lively expenses, affecting taking care of ways of behaving, scrounging methodologies, and in general life history attributes. Compromises among speed and perseverance, mobility and security, and
   the requests of various environmental specialties force imperatives
   on locomotor variations. Understanding these difficulties gives an
   all encompassing point of view on the complexities of vertebrate
   development.
2. Human Effect and Protection Concerns

Human exercises, including territory obliteration, contamination, and
environmental change, present critical difficulties to vertebrate headway. Preservation concerns emerge as species face disturbances to their
regular development designs, territory fracture, and expanded dangers of
eradication. Perceiving the effect of human exercises on vertebrate movement is fundamental for creating powerful preservation methodologies
that offset human requirements with biological uprightness.

B. Significance of Studying Locomotion Diversity

The investigation of motion variety in the animals of the world collectively fills in as a door to understanding the unpredictable variations that
have developed more than great many years. Velocity, the capacity to
move starting with one spot then onto the next, is a key part of a living
being's science, personally connected to endurance, proliferation, and
natural communications.

The meaning of digging into the assorted manners by which creatures
move stretches out past simple interest, offering significant experiences

into developmental cycles, natural elements, and likely applications in different fields.

1. Unwinding Transformative Accounts: Experiences from Motion
1. Transformative Variations and Advancements
   The variety in velocity methodologies across various creature bunches uncovers an embroidery of transformative variations and developments. From the undulating developments of fish balances to the taking off trips of birds, each locomotor technique mirrors the particular tensions and biological specialties that formed the transformative direction of species. Concentrating on headway variety gives a window into the transformative narratives of living beings, permitting researchers to follow the beginnings of remarkable variations and comprehend the elements driving their turn of events.
2. Momentary Minutes and Developmental Changes

Momentary crossroads throughout the entire existence of life, for example, the shift from water to land or the advancement of flight, are unpredictably attached to headway transformations. Concentrating on these changes gives essential bits of knowledge into the difficulties life forms confronted and the arrangements that arose through normal determination. The investigation of how blades changed into appendages or how plumes empowered flight divulges the amazing pliancy of life and the powerful idea of transformative cycles.

II. Biological Elements: Adjusting to Assorted Conditions

1. Living space Specialization and Specialty Inhabitance
   The locomotor variations of living beings are finely tuned to the particular requests of their surroundings, mirroring their environmental jobs and techniques for endurance. Species adjusted for amphibian motion might display smoothed out bodies and blades advanced for submerged development, while earthly experts may grandstand appendage structures custom fitted for exploring shifted scenes. Understanding movement variety permits scientists to disentangle the complexities of specialty inhabitance and how various species have particular to take advantage of explicit natural surroundings.
2. Hunter Prey Elements and Rummaging Methodologies

The investigation of velocity variety adds to our perception of hunter prey elements and rummaging techniques inside environments. The pursuit capacities of hunters, the sly moves of prey, and the assorted manners by which living beings look for food are totally entwined with their locomotor transformations.

These elements shape the harmony between environments and impact the conveyance and overflow of species, eventually influencing biodiversity at different trophic levels.

III. Biomechanical Wonders: Structure, Capability, and Effectiveness

1. Biomechanics of Motion

The biomechanics of motion dive into the perplexing interaction between a creature's structure and its useful transformations for development. From the effective hydrodynamics of fish balances to the streamlined wonders of bird wings, biomechanics gives a quantitative comprehension of how organic entities beat actual difficulties to accomplish ideal locomotor productivity. The investigation of headway biomechanics has functional applications, moving advancements in mechanical technology, designing, and plan.

2. Productivity Compromises and Limitations

Each locomotor transformation accompanies intrinsic compromises and limitations. Species upgraded for speed might forfeit perseverance, while those adjusted for security might think twice about. Investigating these compromises improves how we might interpret the different arrangements that have advanced to address explicit locomotor difficulties. Unwinding the requirements forced by various conditions gives important bits of knowledge into the constraints of locomotor variations and the trade offs organic entities make to flourish in their natural specialties.

IV. Applications in Biomimicry: Nature as a Plan Motivation

1. Biomimicry and Mechanical Advancement

The investigation of motion variety has direct applications in biomimicry, where nature's plans motivate mechanical advancements. Specialists and creators frequently shift focus over to the effectiveness and style of normal velocity transformations to educate the creation regarding robots, vehicles, and gadgets. From fish-enlivened submerged robots to bird-impersonating airplane, biomimicry outfits the insight of development to tackle complex designing difficulties and enhance the exhibition of human-made frameworks.

2. Bio-propelled Advanced mechanics and Prosthetics

Propels in bio-enlivened mechanical technology draw vigorously from the standards of motion variety. Advanced mechanics that imitate the developments of creatures, for example, snake-like robots for investigation or quadrupedal robots for harsh landscape, benefit from the biomechanical illustrations learned through the investigation of regular headway. Furthermore, the advancement of prosthetics and exoskeletons frequently takes motivation from the effective appendage designs and joint developments saw in different creature species.

V. Protection Suggestions: Saving Versatile Procedures

1. Protection of Biodiversity

   The protection of biodiversity is unpredictably associated with the conservation of headway variety. Species with extraordinary locomotor transformations are frequently particular for explicit territories and environmental specialties. Environment obliteration, environmental change, and human exercises can upset regular development designs, prompting populace declines and even annihilations. Concentrating on movement variety adds to preservation endeavors by featuring the significance of protecting environments that help a great many locomotor procedures.

2. Sign of Environment Wellbeing

The investigation of velocity variety can act as a mark of environment wellbeing. Changes in locomotor ways of behaving, relocation examples, or scrounging methodologies might flag disturbances inside environments. Observing motion transformations gives specialists significant information to evaluate the effect of ecological changes on species and biological systems, supporting the advancement of informed protection techniques.

C. Evolutionary Perspective on Vertebrate Locomotion

The development of vertebrate movement remains as a demonstration of the unique interaction among creatures and their consistently evolving conditions. Throughout the span of millions of years, vertebrates have expanded into a huge number of environmental specialties, each requesting interesting procedures for development and endurance. This investigation digs into the developmental points of view on vertebrate velocity, following the pathways of versatile advancement that have prompted the staggering variety of development saw across fish, creatures of land and water, reptiles, birds, and warm blooded animals.

1. Fish: Trailblazers of Amphibian Headway
1. Starting points of Fish Headway
   The excursion of vertebrate motion starts in the watery domains

where fish, the trailblazers of oceanic development, advanced. The earliest fish explored the oceans with crude balances, making way for the resulting development of assorted locomotor variations. The undulating developments of fish bodies, combined with the improvement of different blade structures, worked with proficient drive through water and denoted a huge achievement in the transformative timetable.

2. Variety in Fish Velocity

The variety in fish velocity is a demonstration of the versatile radiations that happened in sea-going conditions. From the smoothed out assemblages of quick swimming hunters like sharks to the intricate balance plans of beam finned fish, every species advanced locomotor transformations custom-made to its biological specialty. Understanding the transformative variety in fish motion gives bits of knowledge into the particular tensions driving the advancement of explicit development procedures.

II. Creatures of land and water: Exploring The two Universes

1. Developmental Changes to Earthbound Life
The change from water to land denoted a urgent second in vertebrate development, and creatures of land and water arose as the trailblazers of earthly movement. Appendages developed from balances, empowering them to explore both amphibian and earthbound conditions. The land and water proficient life cycle, with its oceanic hatchlings and earthbound grown-ups, exhibits the flexibility of locomotor procedures in light of evolving environments.

2. Appendage Variety in Creatures of land and water

The variety in appendage structures among creatures of land and water mirrors the fluctuated environmental specialties they possess. From the strong rear appendages of jumping frogs to the smoothed out collections of oceanic lizards, creatures of land and water have developed a scope of locomotor variations. The appendage changes in creatures of land and water give a focal point through which to grasp the developmental developments that worked with the victory of earthly conditions.

III. Reptiles: Vanquishing Area and Sky

1. Tetrapod Advances and Appendage Specialization
Reptiles, the following part in vertebrate development, further refined the change to earthbound life. Appendages went through additional specialization, and reptiles expanded into different structures

adjusted to vanquish both land and air. The development of rambling and erect appendage stances, found in reptiles and dinosaurs, separately, embodies the assorted pathways taken by reptiles in their victory of earthbound living spaces.

2. Airborne Advancements in Pterosaurs and Birds

The development of trip in reptiles saw surprising advancements, especially in pterosaurs and birds. Pterosaurs, the flying reptiles of the Mesozoic time, created wingspans equaling those of current birds. The ensuing development of fueled trip in birds presented feathers, empty bones, and concentrated wing structures.

The equal advancement of trip in these two gatherings grandstands the concurrent pathways to ethereal motion inside the reptilian ancestry.

IV. Warm blooded animals: Earthbound Dominance and Then some

1. Mammalian Variety in Earthly Velocity
Warm blooded animals, with their different variations, have made unmatched progress in earthly velocity. From the cursorial variations of cheetahs to the strong appendages of herbivores, vertebrates exhibit many locomotor techniques. Furthermore, marine vertebrates like dolphins and whales have developed smoothed out bodies and flippers for effective amphibian velocity. The developmental variety in mammalian headway mirrors the environmental adaptability of this class of vertebrates.

2. Advancement of Bipedalism in People

The development of bipedalism in hominins addresses an exceptional direction in mammalian headway. The shift from quadrupedalism to bipedalism in early hominins denoted a critical takeoff from the locomotor examples of their primate family members. The physical variations related with bipedalism, for example, a completely upstanding stance and changes in appendage structure, empowered hominins to investigate new biological specialties and in the long run led to Homo sapiens.

V. Shared Standards and Joined Development

1. Biomechanical Standards in Vertebrate Headway
Certain biomechanical standards underlie vertebrate headway, filling in as consistent ideas woven through the embroidered artwork of transformative variety. The planned developments of muscles, the influence given by skeletal designs, and the streamlining of energy

consumption are shared rules that add to the proficiency of locomotor transformations across different vertebrate gatherings.

2. Concurrent Development in Locomotor Transformations

Concurrent development is a repetitive topic in vertebrate headway, where comparable transformations advance freely in various heredities. The smoothed out groups of dolphins and ichthyosaurs, the cursorial transformations of cheetahs and ostriches, and the airborne capacities of bats and birds embody the combination of locomotor procedures because of comparable particular tensions. Concurrent development features the adaptability of arrangements that emerge to address the difficulties of explicit natural settings.

VI. Developmental Advancements: Quills, Appendages, and Then some

1. The Advancement of Quills
   Feathers, at first advanced for protection and show in non-avian dinosaurs, went through additional adjustments that made ready for the development of controlled trip in birds. The improvement of flight feathers with unbalanced vanes and the presence of a fall for muscle connection are key developments that empowered birds to accomplish supported flight. Feathers, initially a result of sexual choice, became instrumental in the transformative outcome of avian movement.

2. Appendage Developments in Earthly Variations

The development of appendages addresses a sign of vertebrate movement, with different advancements taking care of explicit biological requests. From the prehensile appendages of primates for tree-staying to the hoofed appendages of ungulates for fast earthly development, appendage structures have adjusted to a bunch of capabilities. The developmental advancements in appendage morphology outline the powerful exchange among structure and capability in light of specific tensions.

VII. Imperatives, Difficulties, and Versatile Reactions

1. Lively Expenses and Compromises
   The productivity of movement accompanies related lively expenses and compromises. Species adjusted for speed might forfeit perseverance, while those enhanced for solidness might think twice about. Understanding these compromises gives bits of knowledge into the

perplexing choices creatures set to adjust clashing expectations forced by their surroundings.

2. Challenges in Changing Conditions

The changes among oceanic and earthbound conditions, or among land and air, present special difficulties for vertebrates. The development of specific locomotor transformations frequently concurs with momentary minutes, where species explore new environmental specialties. The difficulties of progressing conditions drive the versatile reactions that shape the locomotor variety saw in various vertebrate heredities.

VIII. Future Viewpoints: Incorporating Developmental Bits of knowledge

1. Coordinating Developmental Science and Movement Studies
   The mix of developmental science and headway studies gives a comprehensive comprehension of how vertebrates have adjusted to their surroundings throughout transformative time. Developmental bits of knowledge upgrade our enthusiasm for the unique cycles that have molded locomotor variety and open roads for investigating the interconnectedness of structure, capability, and environmental setting.
2. Innovative and Clinical Applications

The experiences acquired from concentrating on the developmental viewpoints on vertebrate motion have reasonable applications in different fields. Biomimicry, enlivened essentially's plans, keeps on driving advancements in mechanical technology, prosthetics, and designing. The comprehension of transformative variations likewise adds to clinical fields, illuminating the improvement regarding restoration methodologies and intercessions for people with portability challenges.

Chapter 1

Fish: Fins and Efficient Aquatic Locomotion

Fish, with their exceptional variety and versatility, have developed a wide exhibit of highlights that empower them to flourish in oceanic conditions. One of the most basic parts of their variation is the improvement of blades, specific limbs that assume a vital part in their proficient motion submerged. This far reaching investigation dives into the life systems, usefulness, and transformative meaning of fish blades, revealing insight into how these designs add to the surprising swimming capacities of fish.

Life systems of Fish Balances:

Kinds of Balances:

Fish have different kinds of balances, each filling a particular need in their motion. These incorporate dorsal blades, pectoral balances, pelvic balances, butt-centric balances, and caudal blades. Understanding the life systems and capability of each balance is critical to unwinding the complexities of fish impetus.

Dorsal Balances:

Situated on the fish's back, dorsal blades give strength during swimming. Their level and shape can change among species, affecting the fish's capacity to make speedy moves and keep up with balance.

Pectoral Balances:

Situated on one or the other side of the fish, pectoral balances are fundamental for directing and keeping up with horizontal strength. The scope of movement and adaptability of pectoral balances are demonstrative of a fish's moving capacities.

Pelvic Balances:

Found on the ventral side of the fish, pelvic balances help with keeping up with profundity and soundness. They add to the general coordination of developments, particularly during slow and exact moves.

Butt-centric Blades:

Situated on the fish's ventral side close to the tail, butt-centric blades help in forestalling moving movements. They work pair with different blades to guarantee smoothed out development through the water.

Caudal Balances:

The caudal balance, or tail blade, is ostensibly the most urgent for drive. It moves the fish forward and is profoundly factor in shape, mirroring the swimming propensities and way of life of various fish species.

Utilitarian Parts of Fish Blades:

Hydrodynamics of Balances:

The shape and design of fish balances are finely tuned to proficiently associate with water. The standards of hydrodynamics, including lift, drag, and push, are fundamental in understanding how balances move fish through the water with negligible energy consumption.

Pectoral Balances and Mobility:

The pectoral balances, with their expansive surface region and fine control, assume a pivotal part in a fish's capacity to make speedy turns and explore complex conditions. The mechanics of these blades add to the fish's general nimbleness.

Caudal Blades and Impetus:

The variety in caudal balance shapes, going from forked to lunate, impacts a fish's swimming style and speed. Different caudal balance types are adjusted to explicit natural specialties, giving a brief look into the developmental tensions molding fish movement.

Variations for Various Conditions:

Fish have adjusted their balances to different amphibian conditions, from quick waterways to open seas. Looking at these transformations gives bits of knowledge into the connection among structure and capability in fish blade advancement.

Developmental Points of view:

Developmental Starting points of Blades:

Following the transformative history of fish balances uncovers their progressive improvement from tribal vertebrates. The change from lobed balances to the particular blades found in present day fish is a demonstration of the specific tensions forced by various oceanic conditions.

Blades as Versatile Arrangements:

The variety of blade types and shapes across fish species highlights the versatility of balances as developmental answers for explicit difficulties. Inspecting how balances have advanced permits researchers to induce the biological settings that molded fish motion.

Joined Development in Fish Blades:

Joined development, where comparative qualities advance freely in various heredities, is obvious in the blades of remotely related fish species. This peculiarity gives important bits of knowledge into the practical benefits of explicit blade types in various conditions.

Human Applications and Biomimicry:

Concentrating on fish blades has commonsense applications, motivating advancements in submerged mechanical technology and biomimetic plan. Designers and scientists draw motivation from the proficiency of fish balances to foster more dexterous and energy-productive submerged vehicles.

1.1 Overview of Fish Locomotion

Fish, as occupants of oceanic conditions, have developed different and effective systems for motion to explore their environmental elements, catch prey, and stay away from hunters. This outline investigates the different techniques for fish headway, underscoring the job of balances in making a bunch of swimming styles. From the undulating developments of eels to the fast eruptions of speed displayed by fish, fish have created locomotor methodologies that feature the wonders of transformative variation.

Body and Muscle Transformations:

Fish show a smoothed out body shape that decreases drag and improves their capacity to effectively travel through water. The fusiform body configuration, frequently alluded to as obliterate molded, limits opposition and is normal among quick swimming species. Moreover, the muscular build of fish is adjusted for fast and strong withdrawals, considering quick developments and speedy reactions to changes in the climate.

Undulatory Headway:

Undulatory motion is a typical method of swimming among fish, described by cadenced sidelong developments of the body. This sort of velocity is common in species like eels and lampreys. The undulating waves made by the fish's body spread from head to tail, driving the fish forward. The level of shape in the waves and the recurrence of withdrawals add to varieties in swimming rate and readiness.

Oscillatory Movement:

Oscillatory headway includes the volatile development of the body, normally utilized by species with prolonged bodies and dorsal and butt-centric balances. This sort of velocity is seen in fish like angelfish and seahorses, where the dorsal and butt-centric balances assume a critical part in adjustment and guiding. The musical motions permit these fish to keep up with exact command over their developments.

MediFin Drive:

Some fish utilize an interesting method of velocity known as middle or dorsal blade impetus. This includes the undulation of the dorsal balance, making push that moves the fish forward. Species, for example, knifefish and specific sorts of catfish utilize this technique, exhibiting the adaptability of blade structures in fish headway.

Pectoral Balance Paddling:

Pectoral balance paddling is a strategy for headway described by the musical development of pectoral blades, looking like the paddling movement of paddles. Flying fish are outstanding specialists of this style, using their amplified pectoral blades to coast over the water's surface. This transformation empowers them to cover critical distances while avoiding hunters.

Stream Impetus:

A few fish, like the octopus and cuttlefish, use stream impetus for quick development. This includes the removal of water through a siphon, creating a power that impels the fish the other way. While not rigorously balance based, fly impetus grandstands the different locomotor systems utilized by oceanic life forms.

Caudal Blade Drive:

Caudal blade drive is a transcendent method of swimming among fish, where the tail balance, or caudal blade, is the essential wellspring of pushed. The shape and construction of the caudal blade shift altogether among species, impacting their swimming capacities. From the forked tails of quick swimming fish to the strong, bow formed tails of sharks, the caudal blade is a critical determinant of swimming style.

Lightness and Swim Bladders:

Fish likewise use lightness to control their situation in the water section. Numerous species have swim bladders, gas-filled organs that permit them to change their lightness by controlling the volume of gas. This transformation is urgent for keeping up with profundity and rationing energy during various periods of swimming.

Ecological Transformations:

The decision of locomotor system frequently mirrors the particular natural specialty involved by a fish animal types. For instance, fish in quick streaming waterways might foster smoothed out bodies and strong tails to explore against ebbs and flows, while those in coral reefs might depend on exact moves and oscillatory developments among complex designs.

Vivacious Contemplations:

Fish motion is innately attached to energy consumption. Species have advanced methodologies to adjust the requirement for effective development with the protection of energy. The changing metabolic requests of various locomotor styles add to the variety of swimming systems saw across fish taxa.

Hunter Prey Elements:

The proficiency of fish movement is unpredictably connected to hunter prey elements. Ruthless fish frequently display burst swimming abilities for quick quest for prey, while prey species might depend on deftness, cover, or quick break systems. Understanding these elements gives bits of knowledge into the coevolutionary weapons contest among hunters and their prey.

1.2 Diversity in Fin Structures

The variety of blade structures among fish is a demonstration of the mind boggling versatility and development of sea-going living beings. Blades fill a large number of needs, including impetus, dependability, and mobility, and their varieties across species are an impression of the interesting environmental specialties involved by various fish. This far reaching investigation digs into the bunch types of blades tracked down in the amphibian domain, looking at the transformative drivers behind their variety and the utilitarian specializations that empower fish to flourish in different conditions.

Transformative Beginnings of Blades:

The development of blades is well established in the progress from oceanic vertebrates to the different cluster of fish species we notice today. The hereditary blades of early vertebrates were possible basic projections utilized for adjustment and equilibrium. After some time, these designs went through huge changes, prompting the improvement of specific balances with unmistakable capabilities.

Dorsal Blades:

1. Adjustment and Hydrodynamics:
   Dorsal blades, situated along the midline of a fish's back, assume a urgent part in adjustment and hydrodynamics. Their level and shape shift generally among species, impacting a fish's capacity to keep up with equilibrium and make quick moves. The dorsal blade is many times the first to arise during undeveloped turn of events, displaying its essential job in fish velocity.
2. Capability in Various Conditions:

In some fish, the dorsal balance might have a more stretched and sail-like appearance, giving solidness in vast water. Conversely, species occupying complex conditions might have more modest, more adaptable dorsal blades that guide in exact moving among snags.

Pectoral Blades:

1. Controlling and Mobility:
   Pectoral blades, situated on one or the other side of a fish's body, are essential for guiding and mobility. The scope of movement and adaptability of pectoral blades fluctuate across species, impacting a fish's capacity to make difficult maneuvers, float set up, and explore unpredictable conditions.
2. Variations for Various Ways of life:

Pectoral balances are adjusted to suit the ways of life of various fish. In species that abide close the ocean bottom, these blades might be adjusted into appendage like designs, supporting base dwelling exercises. Flying fish, then again, have extended pectoral balances that empower them to coast over the water surface.
Pelvic Blades:

1. Keeping up with Profundity and Steadiness:
   Pelvic blades, situated on the ventral side of a fish close to the pelvic support, add to keeping up with profundity and steadiness. Their job is especially vital during slow and exact developments, where the fish needs to change its situation without exhausting unreasonable energy.
2. Varieties in Pelvic Balance Construction:

Pelvic balances show significant varieties in structure, going from little and minimal in certain species to prolonged and exceptionally portable in others. These variations mirror the particular necessities of the fish's territory and conduct.
Butt-centric Blades:

1. Forestalling Moving Movements:
   Butt-centric blades, situated on the ventral side close to the tail, add to forestalling moving movements. Working collaborating with different blades, especially the dorsal balance, butt-centric blades assume a part in keeping up with the fish's steadiness during swim-ming.
2. Job in Regenerative Ways of behaving:

In specific fish species, butt-centric balances might assume a part in conceptive ways of behaving, with guys creating particular designs for romance shows or home structure exercises.

Caudal Balances:

1. Drive and Swimming Styles:
   The caudal balance, or tail blade, is seemingly the most basic for impetus and decides a fish's swimming style. The state of the caudal blade fluctuates widely among species and is characteristic of their environmental specialty, speed prerequisites, and way of life.
2. Heterocercal versus Homocercal Tails:
   Fish might have heterocercal tails, where the upper curve is bigger than the lower curve (e.g., sharks), or homocercal tails, where the curves are of equivalent size (e.g., roost). These varieties are connected to the fish's lightness, speed, and mobility in various seagoing conditions.
3. Concentrated Caudal Blade Transformations:

Some fish show specific transformations of the caudal balance. Fish, for example, have a bow molded caudal blade that empowers quick eruptions of speed, while angelfish might have an adjusted caudal balance that upgrades mobility in complex reef conditions.

Practical Variety in Fish Movement:

1. Hydrodynamics and Effectiveness:
   The variety in balance structures mirrors the perplexing exchange of hydrodynamics and proficiency in fish velocity. Various blades add to lift, push, and drag in remarkable ways, enhancing the fish's capacity to travel through water with negligible energy consumption.
2. Swimming Styles and Environmental Variations:

Fish show many swimming styles, from the strong and quick swimming of pelagic species to the exact and sluggish developments of benthic tenants. These styles are intently attached to the fish's environmental specialty, taking care of propensities, and reaction to predation pressures.

Focalized Development in Blade Designs:

1. Comparative Answers for Environmental Difficulties:
   Focalized development is obvious in fish species that are not firmly related yet share comparative environmental difficulties. The improvement of practically equivalent to blade structures because of

comparable ecological requests features the proficiency of specific transformations in unambiguous settings.

2. Instances of United Development:

The smoothed out bodies and fusiform shapes saw in quick swimming species, like fish and dolphins, exhibit joined advancement in light of the requirement for speed and mobility in vast water conditions.

Natural Impacts on Blade Development:

1. Ecomorphology and Living space Transformations:
   The investigation of ecomorphology investigates how the communication between a creature and its current circumstance shapes its morphology. Fish blades embody ecomorphological transformations, with varieties in balance structures mirroring the particular difficulties presented by various amphibian natural surroundings.
2. Coral Reefs, Waterways, and Open Seas:

Fish occupying coral reefs might have blades adjusted for exact moving among coral arrangements, while those in quick streaming waterways might have balances helpful for exploring solid ebbs and flows. Vast sea inhabitants, then again, may have balances streamlined for extremely long travel.

Biomechanics of Balance Usefulness:

1. Muscle Plan and Balance Control:
   The biomechanics of balance usefulness include the course of action of muscles and the unpredictable control instruments that permit fish to adjust the shape and development of their blades. Understanding these biomechanics gives bits of knowledge into the proficiency of fish movement.
2. Adaptability and Inflexibility:

Blades might display fluctuating levels of adaptability and unbending nature, affecting their part in various parts of fish velocity. Exceptionally adaptable blades, for instance, add to calibrated controlling and nimbleness, while unbending balances might be more viable in producing push for quick swimming.

Effect of Natural Change on Balance Advancement:

1. Versatility and Pliancy:
   Fish balances feature flexibility and versatility in light of changing

natural circumstances. Developmental changes in blade designs might happen throughout lengthy time scales, while phenotypic versatility permits fish to change their balance shapes and works inside their lifetimes.

2. Human-Initiated Changes:

Anthropogenic variables, for example, environmental change and territory debasement, can impact the specific tensions on fish populaces, possibly prompting versatile changes in balance structures. Understanding these elements is significant for preservation endeavors and maintainable administration of sea-going environments.

Biomimicry and Mechanical Applications:

1. Motivation for Designing:
   The investigation of fish balance variety has roused specialists to create bio-motivated advances. Biomimicry of fish blades has prompted the formation of additional proficient submerged vehicles and robots equipped for exploring complex oceanic conditions.
2. Hydrodynamic Plan in Mechanical technology:

Analysts have drawn upon the hydrodynamic standards saw in fish blades to plan mechanical balances that improve lift, push, and drag. These developments have suggestions for submerged investigation, reconnaissance, and ecological checking.

1.3 Mechanisms of Propulsion in Fish

Fish, as experts of sea-going conditions, have developed a different exhibit of components for impetus, permitting them to explore, chase, and break with momentous productivity. Drive in fish is a mind boggling transaction of biomechanics, muscle physiology, and hydrodynamics, with different variations that take care of the particular necessities of various species. This investigation digs into the complexities of impetus systems in fish, revealing insight into how these organic entities have improved their skills to travel through water with unrivaled accuracy and speed.

Muscle Constriction and Body Adaptability:

1. Myotomal Muscles:
   The essential power behind fish drive lies in the cadenced compression of myotomal muscles, which are organized in a progression of W-molded fragments along the body. These muscles produce undulatory waves that movement from head to tail, driving the

fish forward. The recurrence and abundancy of muscle constrictions shift among species, impacting swimming rate and deftness.

2. Metameric Division:
   The metameric division of myotomal muscles takes into consideration a consecutive, wave-like movement. This game plan guarantees a consistent and proficient exchange of energy starting with one muscle portion then onto the next, empowering supported swimming over significant distances.

3. Red Muscle versus White Muscle:

Fish have both red and white muscle filaments, each fit to various swimming modes. Red muscle filaments are wealthy in oxygen-conveying myoglobin and are adjusted for maintained, vigorous swimming. Conversely, white muscle strands, which are anaerobic and produce fast explosions of force, are used for speedy speed increases and escapes.

Undulatory Motion:

1. Wavelike Developments:
   Undulatory motion is the most well-known type of fish impetus, portrayed by the engendering of wavelike developments along the body. The undulatory waves are produced by the horizontal bowing of the body, started by the constriction of myotomal muscles on one side and followed by the unwinding of muscles on the contrary side.

2. Plentifulness and Recurrence Control:
   Fish have exact command over the sufficiency and recurrence of undulatory developments, permitting them to change their swimming way of behaving as indicated by ecological circumstances, the presence of hunters or prey, and the requirement for energy protection.

3. Tail Beat and Push Age:

The undulatory movement comes full circle in a tail beat, where the caudal blade delivers a propulsive push. The shape and design of the caudal blade, joined with the undulatory movement, add to the making of forward push and effective swimming.

Caudal Blade Morphology and Capability:

1. Heterocercal and Homocercal Tails:
   The morphology of the caudal blade is a basic determinant of a fish's swimming style. Heterocercal tails, where the upper curve is bigger than the lower curve, are in many cases found in quick swimming species like sharks. Homocercal tails, with equivalent estimated

curves, are regular in hard fish and add to a harmony among speed and mobility.

2. **Lunate, Forked, and Adjusted Tails:**
   Inside homocercal tails, varieties, for example, lunate, forked, and adjusted shapes further impact swimming capacities. Lunate tails, looking like a bow, are related with quick swimmers like fish, while forked tails are found in species requiring dexterity. Adjusted tails are seen in more slow moving fish, adding to steadiness.

3. **Job of the Caudal Peduncle:**

The caudal peduncle, the limited district associating the body to the caudal balance, assumes a critical part in blade development and control. Its adaptability and muscle structure add to the tweaking of swimming developments and changes because of natural elements.

Pectoral Balance Paddling and Oscillatory Developments:

1. **Paddling Movement of Pectoral Balances:**
   In some fish, especially flying fish, pectoral blades are adjusted for a paddling movement. The pectoral balances move in a planned way, looking like the paddling of paddles, permitting the fish to skim over the water's surface. This variation empowers flying fish to cover huge distances while getting away from hunters.

2. **Oscillatory Developments for Accuracy:**

Oscillatory developments include to and fro movement, frequently saw in species exploring complex conditions. Fish with stretched bodies, like seahorses and pipefish, use oscillatory developments for exact moving among structures like corals and vegetation.

Fly Impetus in Cephalopods:

1. **Siphon and Water Ejection:**
   Cephalopods, including octopuses and squids, utilize an exceptional type of impetus known as stream drive. This includes the compression of mantle muscles to compel water through a siphon, making a fly that impels the creature the other way. Fly impetus is especially powerful for quick escapes and exact developments.

2. **Mobility and Speed:**

The capacity to quickly change the course and power of the stream permits cephalopods to display momentous mobility. This drive technique is exceptionally powerful in vast water and gives an upper hand in both hunter prey communications and keeping away from expected dangers.

Hydrodynamic Collaborations and Lift Age:

1. Communication with Water:
   The effectiveness of fish drive is complicatedly attached to hydrodynamic connections between the fish and water. Balances are intended to limit drag, and the undulatory developments of the body make lift, permitting fish to keep up with lightness and control their profundity in the water segment.
2. Hydrofoil Impact of Balances:
   Balances capability as hydrofoils, producing lift as water streams over and under their surfaces. This lift adds to the general push and forward movement of the fish. The size, shape, and direction of blades are finely tuned to enhance the hydrofoil impact for various swimming styles.
3. Lightness and Swim Bladders:

Lightness control is fundamental for fish impetus, and numerous species have swim bladders that assist with managing their situation in the water segment. By changing the volume of gas inside the swim bladder, fish can accomplish impartial lightness, moderating energy during different periods of swimming.

Natural Effects on Impetus:

1. Flows and Water Stream:
   Fish adjust their drive instruments to explore different water conditions, including quick streaming streams, open seas, and stale lakes. The connection among fish and water flows impacts the energy consumption and proficiency of their swimming developments.
2. Base Dwelling and Benthic Transformations:

Base dwelling species might show specific variations for impetus in substrate-rich conditions. Adaptable bodies and concentrated blades empower these fish to explore and scrounge among rocks, sand, and vegetation with accuracy.

Hunter Prey Elements and Burst Swimming:

1. Burst Swimming for Pursuit and Departure:
   Hunter prey elements apply critical tension on fish drive transformations. Ruthless fish frequently display burst swimming abilities,

permitting them to seek after and catch prey quickly. Then again, prey species foster procedures for fast escapes, depending on lithe developments and quick speed increases.

2. Particular Designs for Predation:

Some fish species have developed specific designs, like prolonged jaws or toothed mouths, to upgrade their savage abilities. These transformations are supplemented by productive impetus instruments that work with compelling hunting procedures.

Versatile Changes and Phenotypic Pliancy:

1. Transformative Reactions to Natural Movements:
   Throughout developmental time scales, fish populaces might go through versatile changes because of movements in their current circumstance. Regular choice follows up on characteristics connected with impetus, leaning toward those that improve endurance and regenerative outcome in unambiguous environmental specialties.
2. Phenotypic Pliancy and Acclimatization:

Phenotypic pliancy permits individual fish to adapt to changing ecological circumstances inside their lifetimes. This pliancy might include adjustments in muscle movement, blade morphology, or swimming way of behaving to streamline drive in light of shifting natural difficulties.

Biomimicry and Mechanical Applications:

1. Bio-Motivation for Mechanical technology:
   The investigation of fish drive instruments has enlivened the plan of submerged advanced mechanics and independent vehicles. Engineers draw upon the effectiveness and adaptability saw in fish headway to make bio-propelled advances equipped for exploring complex submerged conditions.
2. Hydrodynamic Proficiency in Submarines:

Subs and submerged vehicles benefit from the investigation of fish hydrodynamics to improve their productivity. The biomimetic plan of blades and drive frameworks adds to the improvement of vehicles equipped for exact moves and smoothed out developments.

1.4 Evolutionary Transitions in Fish Locomotion

The transformative excursion of fish motion is an enthralling story of variation, development, and the determined drive of life to investigate and vanquish sea-going conditions. More than great many years, fish have gone through exceptional changes in their locomotor techniques, from the basic undulations of hereditary structures to the improvement of blades and, now and again, even the rise of simple appendages. This developmental story offers a brief look into the powerful cycles that have formed the variety of fish velocity we notice today.

Undulatory Headway in Early Vertebrates:

The earliest vertebrates, reasonable looking like jawless fishes, depended on undulatory headway as an essential method for swimming. The undulations of the body permitted these crude vertebrates to explore water and seek after prey effectively. While coming up short on the specific blades found in current fish, these early structures established the groundwork for the transformative advancements that would follow.

Improvement of Pectoral and Pelvic Balances:

As vertebrates kept on advancing, the improvement of matched blades denoted a critical achievement in fish headway. Pectoral and pelvic blades arose, giving another degree of control and mobility. The pectoral blades, situated on one or the other side of the body, assumed a urgent part in guiding and parallel solidness, while the pelvic balances added to keeping up with profundity and steadiness.

Transformative Meaning of Dorsal and Butt-centric Balances:

The expansion of dorsal and butt-centric blades further improved the solidness and hydrodynamic effectiveness of fish. Situated along the dorsal and ventral midlines, separately, these blades forestalled moving movements and added to the general coordination of developments. The development of these balances permitted fish to investigate a more extensive scope of sea-going conditions, from tempestuous streams to open seas.

Caudal Blade Advancements:

The caudal blade, or tail balance, went through striking transformative developments, turning into a focal part of fish impetus. Early fish probably had heterocercal tails, where the upper curve was bigger than the lower curve, giving lift and solidness. Over the long haul, a few animal groups developed homocercal tails, adding to a more adjusted plan reasonable for a different cluster of swimming styles.

Caudal Blade Variety and Versatile Radiation:

The variety in caudal blade shapes turned into a vital element in the versatile radiation of fish into different biological specialties. Forked tails advanced in species requiring exact moves, like those exploring coral reefs, while lunate tails became normal for quick swimming untamed sea hunters like fish. The assortment in caudal blade morphology is a demonstration of the versatile reactions of fish to their particular surroundings.

Development of Appendages in Sarcopterygian Fish:

Quite possibly of the most uncommon progress in fish movement happened with the advancement of appendages in sarcopterygian fish. These hard fishes, described by plump lobed balances, prepared for the rise of tetrapods — the principal vertebrates to wander onto land. The progress from blades to appendages denoted a significant crossroads in developmental history, showing the unique exchange among sea-going and earthly conditions.

Tetrapod Appendages and Intrusion of Land:

The improvement of appendages in sarcopterygian fish considered another degree of locomotor adaptability. Blades with hard backings developed into appendages with digits, empowering fish to help their weight and cross earthbound conditions. This shift from sea-going to earthbound life denoted a great jump in developmental history, prompting the rise of creatures of land and water and at last reptiles, birds, and vertebrates.

Assembly in Balance and Appendage Usefulness:

Regardless of the difference between fish balances and tetrapod appendages, certain practical similitudes have been distinguished. The undulatory developments of fish blades share likenesses with the appendage developments of strolling tetrapods, demonstrating concurrent advancement in locomotor methodologies. This combination highlights the proficiency of certain biomechanical standards in adjusting to the difficulties presented by various conditions.

Overcoming any issues: Sea-going Tetrapods:

A few tetrapods, even after the colonization of land, held variations for sea-going life. Amphibian tetrapods, like whales and dolphins, feature the adaptability of appendage development. Appendages changed into smoothed out flippers, permitting these animals to explore the sea with effortlessness and speed, giving an interesting scaffold among fish and earthbound tetrapods.

Transformative Continuum and Present day Variety:

The transformative changes in fish headway feature a continuum as opposed to a progression of discrete advances. The variety of fish velocity noticed today — from the undulatory developments of eels to the exact balance developments of seahorses — mirrors the complicated transaction of specific tensions and biological open doors that have formed fish advancement over the long haul.

Chapter 2

Amphibians: The Transition from Water to Land

Creatures of land and water address a captivating section in the developmental history of vertebrates, exemplifying the progress from oceanic to earthly life. This gathering, involving frogs, lizards, and caecilians, has effectively adjusted to assorted conditions, displaying a variety of physiological, physical, and social developments. This exhaustive investigation dives into the multi-layered universe of creatures of land and water, following their developmental excursion, explaining the difficulties looked during the progress from water to land, and featuring the remarkable attributes that characterize these enamoring animals.

Developmental Beginnings of Creatures of land and water:

1. Devonian Period and Tetrapod Progenitors:
   The developmental story of creatures of land and water unfurls during the Late Devonian time frame, around quite a while back. Tetrapod precursors, curve finned fishes with appendage like members, wandered into shallow waters and started the change from blades to appendages, making way for the rise of creatures of land and water.
2. Acanthostega and Ichthyostega:

Fossil disclosures, like those of Acanthostega and Ichthyostega, give basic experiences into the beginning phases of tetrapod advancement. These animals had appendage like designs, yet held highlights demonstrative of their sea-going family line, like gills.

Transformations for Earthly Life:

1. Appendage Improvement and Weight Backing:
   The improvement of appendages was an essential transformation that worked with the change to land. Appendages furnished tetrapods with the capacity to help their body weight, explore lopsided territory, and investigate earthbound conditions.
2. Pneumonic Breath:
   The shift to earthly life required variations in breath. Tetrapods created lungs, a vital change that permitted them to remove oxygen from air instead of water. This progress from cutaneous and gill breath denoted a key change in respiratory physiology.
3. Amniotic Eggs and Conceptive Systems:

The development of amniotic eggs addressed a critical advancement. Not at all like the sea-going eggs of their progenitors, amniotic eggs had defensive films that permitted tetrapods to replicate in earthly conditions. This transformation added to the colonization of assorted living spaces.

Variety of Creatures of land and water:

1. Request Anura (Frogs and Amphibians):
   Frogs and frogs, individuals from the request Anura, are maybe the most conspicuous creatures of land and water. Their variations incorporate strong rear appendages for bouncing, webbed feet for swimming, and a scope of vocalizations utilized in correspondence and mating customs.
2. Request Urodela (Lizards and Newts):
   Lizards and newts, characterized under the request Urodela, display a different cluster of body structures and ways of life. Many hold their oceanic hatchlings, while others go through complete transformation. Appendage recovery is a surprising characteristic shown by specific lizard species.
3. Request Apoda (Caecilians):

Caecilians, having a place with the request Apoda, are limbless and look like night crawlers or snakes. These cryptic creatures of land and water basically occupy tropical locales and show extraordinary variations, including specific jaw structures and a one of a kind method of interior treatment.

Transformation: A Key Variation:

1. Larval versus Grown-up Stages:
   Transformation is a characterizing element of numerous creatures of

land and water, including a noticeable change from oceanic hatchlings to earthbound grown-ups. This interaction permits creatures of land and water to take advantage of various biological specialties during different life stages.

2. **Endocrine Control and Hormonal Changes:**
   Transformation is unpredictably managed by endocrine control, with thyroid chemicals assuming a significant part. Hormonal changes organize the advancement of appendages, resorption of the tail, and the progress from gill to lung breath.

3. **Natural Ramifications:**

Transformation has natural ramifications, empowering creatures of land and water to take advantage of assorted environments. Oceanic hatchlings might occupy lakes or streams, while grown-ups adventure onto land, exhibiting the versatility that has added to the outcome of creatures of land and water in different environments.

Physiological Difficulties of Earthly Life:

1. **Drying up and Skin Transformations:**
   The transition to earthly territories presented creatures of land and water to the gamble of parching. Creatures of land and water countered this test through different skin transformations, including the improvement of glandular designs that produce mucous and poisons, assisting with holding dampness and dissuade hunters.

2. **Temperature Guideline:**
   Earthbound conditions present variances in temperature, presenting difficulties for ectothermic creatures like creatures of land and water. Social variations, for example, lolling and looking for cover, permit creatures of land and water to really direct their internal heat level.

3. **Nitrogenous Waste Discharge:**

The change to earthly life required transformations in nitrogenous waste discharge. Creatures of land and water principally discharge nitrogenous waste as urea, a less poisonous compound than smelling salts, permitting them to preserve water in earthbound conditions.

Land and water proficient Tangible Variations:

1. **Visual and Hear-able Insight:**
   Creatures of land and water frequently depend on sharp visual and hear-able faculties for correspondence, prey discovery, and hunter

evasion. Numerous species have particular variations, for example, enormous eyes and vocal sacs, which assume a significant part in their endurance and multiplication.

2. Substance Correspondence:
   Creatures of land and water, especially lizards, utilize substance correspondence through pheromones. These substance signals assume an essential part in mate choice, regional checking, and acknowledgment of conspecifics, adding to the intricacy of land and water proficient social connections.

3. Sidelong Line Framework:

The sidelong line framework, well-developed in oceanic hatchlings, supports recognizing water development and vibrations. While less articulated in earthbound grown-ups, remainders of the horizontal line framework feature the transformative history of creatures of land and water and their oceanic parentage.

Land and water proficient Proliferation and Parental Consideration:

1. Reproducing Methodologies:
   Creatures of land and water display different reproducing techniques. Anuran species, like frogs, frequently take part in unstable rearing occasions where huge numbers gather to imitate. Lizards might utilize romance showcases, and a few animal groups display elaborate mating customs.

2. Egg Affidavit and Parental Consideration:
   Creatures of land and water show a scope of parental consideration ways of behaving. While numerous species lay their eggs in water, others use wet earthbound conditions. A few creatures of land and water monitor their eggs or give parental consideration to hatchlings, guaranteeing their endurance during weak formative stages.

3. Direct Turn of events:

A few creatures of land and water, especially certain types of frogs, go through direct turn of events, bypassing the larval stage out and out. In such cases, eggs hatch into little variants of the grown-ups, bypassing the requirement for a sea-going larval stage.

Creatures of land and water and Natural Connections:

1. Job as Marks of Biological system Wellbeing:
   Creatures of land and water, because of their aversion to natural changes, act as important marks of biological system wellbeing.

Their porous skin makes them defenseless to poisons, and decreases in land and water proficient populaces can flag more extensive biological issues.

2. Taking care of Cooperations:
   Creatures of land and water possess different trophic levels, adding to environment elements. As the two hunters and prey, creatures of land and water assume a part in controlling bug populaces, going about as bioindicators of ecological circumstances.
3. Creatures of land and water and Human Wellbeing:

Creatures of land and water have contributed fundamentally to clinical exploration because of the extraordinary properties of their skin discharges.

Compounds confined from land and water proficient skin have shown expected in drug applications, including the improvement of antimicrobial and pain relieving drugs.

Difficulties and Protection:

1. Territory Misfortune and Discontinuity:
   Creatures of land and water face serious dangers from living space misfortune and discontinuity because of human exercises. Urbanization, deforestation, and rural extension infringe upon their living spaces, restricting their capacity to relocate and track down appropriate rearing destinations.
2. Infection and Arising Microorganisms:
   Creatures of land and water are helpless to arising microorganisms, including the chytrid organism, which has caused wrecking decreases in numerous land and water proficient populaces. Preservation endeavors frequently center around alleviating the effect of illnesses through hostage reproducing programs, environment insurance, and investigation into infection elements.
3. Environmental Change and Land and water proficient Weakness:

Environmental change represents extra difficulties for creatures of land and water, influencing temperature, precipitation examples, and living space accessibility. Species with explicit natural surroundings necessities might confront trouble adjusting to quickly changing ecological circumstances.

Future Viewpoints and Exploration Boondocks:

1. Genomic Studies and Transformative Experiences:
   Propels in genomics have opened new roads for concentrating on the developmental history of creatures of land and water. Similar genomic examinations give bits of knowledge into the hereditary premise of transformations, formative cycles, and the developmental connections among various land and water proficient gatherings.
2. Conduct Environment and Correspondence:
   Conduct nature studies, zeroing in on land and water proficient correspondence, mating ceremonies, and social collaborations, keep on disentangling the intricacies of their way of behaving. Understanding these viewpoints improves our enthusiasm for land and water proficient variety and natural jobs.
3. Preservation Procedures and Local area Inclusion:

Preservation endeavors for creatures of land and water include a mix of environment security, hostage reproducing projects, and public mindfulness crusades.

Local area contribution and resident science drives assume pivotal parts in observing land and water proficient populaces and carrying out powerful preservation measures.

2.1 Evolution of Limbed Locomotion

The development of limbed velocity addresses a vital section throughout the entire existence of vertebrates, denoting the change from seagoing to earthbound conditions. Appendages, at first created as changed balances in fish, went through extraordinary variations that empowered tetrapods (four-limbed vertebrates) to vanquish land and investigate new environmental specialties. This investigation digs into the complicated transformative cycles that formed the improvement of appendages and the assorted methods of earthbound velocity displayed by tetrapods.

Beginnings of Appendages in Fish:

1. Pectoral and Pelvic Blades:
   The transformative excursion of limbed motion can be followed back to the blade to-appendage progress in fish. The earliest tetrapod progenitors probably had altered pectoral and pelvic blades, offering simple help for development in shallow waters. These early appendage like designs established the groundwork for the rise of genuine appendages.
2. Sarcopterygian Fish:

Sarcopterygian fish, a gathering of curve finned fishes, assumed a pivotal part in appendage development. Fossils of sarcopterygians, for example, Eusthenopteron and Panderichthys, show appendage like blades with hard components, indicating the slow change from balances to appendages.

Change to Earthly Life:

1. Devonian Period:
   The Devonian time frame, frequently alluded to as the "Period of Fishes," saw the progress of tetrapod progenitors from amphibian to earthly conditions. The accessibility of new biological specialties and particular tensions in shallow waters probably drove the advancement of appendage like designs that worked with development ashore.
2. Ichthyostega and Acanthostega:

Fossil disclosures of tetrapods like Ichthyostega and Acanthostega give basic bits of knowledge into this change. These early tetrapods held highlights characteristic of their amphibian lineage, including gills and fish-like tails, while displaying appendage transformations for earthly motion.

Early Limbed Motion:

1. Appendages for Help and Development:
   The improvement of appendages in tetrapods gave critical benefits to help and development ashore. Appendages offered a method for raising the body, exploring hindrances, and investigating earthbound conditions. The progress from rambling to more upstanding appendage stances was a huge move toward upgrading velocity.
2. Land and/or water capable Ways of life:
   Early tetrapods probably drove land and/or water capable ways of life, with the capacity to move among sea-going and earthly living spaces. Appendages assumed a double part in swimming and strolling, displaying the flexibility of these designs in adjusting to evolving conditions.
3. Development of Appendage Joints and Skeleton:

The development of appendage joints and a weight-bearing skeleton added to the refinement of earthbound headway. Tetrapods created solid appendage bones, joint explanations that worked with more proficient development, and variations for weight dissemination ashore.

Variety in Appendage Morphology:

1. Anisodactyl and Digitigrade Appendages:
   The development of appendage morphology prompted assorted transformations in appendage structure. Anisodactyl appendages, with digits of shifting lengths, are seen in numerous well evolved creatures, giving a harmony among speed and soundness. Digitigrade appendages, with weight borne on digits, are normal in cursorial species.
2. Plantigrade Appendages:
   Plantigrade appendages, where the whole bottom of the foot connects with the ground, are normal for people and a few primates. This appendage design gives steadiness and a wide base of help, working with exact developments.
3. Cursorial and Graviportal Transformations:

Appendage transformations in cursorial (running) and graviportal (weight-bearing) species grandstand specific highlights. Cursorial transformations, for example, extended appendages, improve speed, while graviportal variations, found in huge well evolved creatures, focus on weight circulation for dependability.

Development of Limbed Headway in Various Tetrapod Gatherings:

1. Reptiles and the Predominance of Rambling Appendages:
   Early reptiles, including rambling reptile like structures, overwhelmed the earthly scene. Rambling appendage act was normal in numerous reptiles, offering dependability yet restricting rate. This appendage setup persevered in a few present day reptiles.
2. Archosaurs and the Change to Raise Appendages:
   The development of archosaurs, including dinosaurs and their relatives, denoted a shift towards an erect appendage pose. Dinosaurs fostered an upstanding position, with appendages situated underneath the body, adding to expanded readiness and the potential for supported speedy development.
3. Mammalian Development and Upstanding Appendages:

Vertebrates developed with a more upstanding appendage pose, a characterizing highlight that recognizes them from different tetrapods. Upstanding appendages considered proficient bipedal velocity in certain species, prompting different methods of development, from jogging to jumping.

Bipedal Velocity:

1. Bipedalism in Dinosaurs and Birds:
   The advancement of bipedalism in dinosaurs, exemplified by theropods, established the groundwork for the improvement of trip in birds. The change of forelimbs into wings exhibited the versatile adaptability of appendage structures, considering both earthly and flying headway.
2. Bipedalism in Warm blooded creatures:

Bipedalism autonomously developed in different mammalian heredities. People, as commit bipeds, show one of a kind transformations in appendage structure, including a noticeable impact point, curved foot, and concentrated joints, working with energy-proficient and perseverance based earthbound motion.

Specific Methods of Limbed Movement:

1. Saltatory Movement:
   Saltatory movement, or bouncing, is seen in different tetrapods, including frogs and kangaroos. Appendages in these species are adjusted for strong drive, underlining solid strength and flexible energy stockpiling for productive bouncing.
2. Cursorial Transformations:
   Cursorial species, adjusted for supported running, show specific appendage structures. Long appendages with diminished digits and stretched metapodials add to a drawn out step length and upgraded speed, found in creatures like cheetahs and ponies.
3. Arboreal Movement:

Arboreal tetrapods, adjusted to life in trees, exhibit different appendage variations. Prehensile appendages, opposable digits, and getting a handle on capacities consider proficient climbing and brachiation. Appendages in arboreal species are many times adaptable, empowering exact developments in complex conditions.

Merged Advancement in Limbed Headway:

1. Instances of Combination:
   Focalized advancement in appendage morphology and motion is apparent across different tetrapod gatherings. Undifferentiated from variations, like smoothed out bodies and appendage arrangements, have advanced freely in species with comparative environmental jobs, representing the force of regular determination in forming versatile arrangements.

2. Morphological Union in Oceanic Conditions:

Combination isn't restricted to earthbound motion; it reaches out to oceanic conditions. Appendage transformations in sea-going tetrapods, like seals and whales, exhibit morphological assembly, with appendages developing into flippers for proficient swimming.
Developmental Meaning of Limbed Motion:

1. Natural Achievement and Living space Colonization:
   Limbed velocity assumed a urgent part in the biological progress of tetrapods. The capacity to continue ashore gave admittance to new food assets, escape from hunters, and colonization of assorted environments, adding to the developmental radiation of tetrapod ancestries.
2. Transformative Arms Races and Hunter Prey Elements:
   Limbed headway affected hunter prey elements, prompting transformative arms races. Pursuit hunters advanced transformations for speed and dexterity, while prey species created systems for avoidance, disguise, or cautious ways of behaving, exhibiting the complex dance of normal determination.
3. Transformative Adaptability and Versatility:

Limbed velocity gave developmental adaptability, permitting tetrapods to adjust to a large number of conditions and biological jobs. This versatility is apparent in the different appendage morphologies and locomotor methodologies saw across tetrapod heredities, featuring the unique idea of developmental cycles.
Future Headings in Limbed Motion Exploration:

1. Propels in Paleontological Revelations:
   Progressing paleontological revelations keep on growing comprehension we might interpret appendage development. Fossil finds, especially in momentary structures, give vital bits of knowledge into the progressive changes that happened during the blade to-appendage change and ensuing variations for earthbound life.
2. Genomic and Formative Investigations:
   Progresses in genomics and formative science offer chances to investigate the hereditary premise of appendage advancement. Relative examinations across tetrapod taxa can uncover the hereditary underpinnings of appendage variety and the sub-atomic pathways engaged with the development of appendage structures.

3. Mix of Biomechanics and Practical Morphology:

Incorporating biomechanical studies with practical morphology upgrades how we might interpret appendage usefulness. Virtual experiences, mechanical technology, and biomechanical demonstrating add to translating the mechanical parts of appendage development and headway, giving an all encompassing point of view on versatile methodologies.

2.2 Adaptations for Terrestrial Locomotion

The change from oceanic to earthly conditions denoted a urgent part in the developmental history of vertebrates. The move from water to land introduced one of a kind difficulties that required the improvement of specific transformations for compelling motion. This investigation digs into the complex cluster of transformations that have developed across assorted taxa, featuring the multi-layered systems utilized by life forms to vanquish earthbound scenes.

Appendages and the Rise of Tetrapods:

1. Balance to-Appendage Change:
   Appendages, at first created as changed balances in fish, assumed a focal part in the progress from oceanic to earthbound motion. The genealogical tetrapod appendage probably emerged through the change of previous balances, giving a way to early tetrapods to explore the difficulties of earthly conditions.

2. Backing and Weight Appropriation:
   Appendages in tetrapods serve for the purpose of drive as well as significant weight-bearing designs. The shift from a level body hub in oceanic precursors to a more upward act considered productive help and weight dispersion, empowering living beings to oppose the draw of gravity ashore.

3. Digit Advancement and Earthbound Transformations:

The advancement of digits, or fingers and toes, added to upgraded earthbound headway. Digits gave a more prominent scope of movement, taking into consideration exact developments and worked on getting a handle on capacities. Earthbound tetrapods developed assorted appendage morphologies, from the spry digits of warm blooded creatures to the mauled appendages of reptiles.

Skeletal Variations for Earthly Headway:

1. Vertebral Section and Hub Skeleton:
   The change to land required variations in the vertebral segment

and pivotal skeleton. The vertebral section offers primary help and adaptability, taking into account proficient movement. Different vertebrate gatherings display varieties in vertebral morphology, reflecting transformations to explicit methods of earthbound development.

2. **Rib Enclosure and Breathing Components:**
The rib confine went through adjustments to work with proficient breathing ashore. Earthly vertebrates created ribcages fit for obliging lungs that remove oxygen from the air. This variation worked on respiratory productivity, a basic element for supported earthbound movement.

3. **Pelvic and Pectoral Supports:**

The pelvic and pectoral supports went through transformations to help the appendage structures and work with successful weight-bearing. Changes in the pelvic support, specifically, assumed a key part in balancing out the rear appendages during earthbound headway, adding to the variety of appendage designs saw in various taxa.

Solid Transformations for Earthbound Movement:

1. **Muscle Plan and Appendage Usefulness:**
The plan of muscles in tetrapod appendages reflects variations for explicit methods of headway. Muscles work in show to give the important power to development, with varieties in muscle connection focuses and fiber direction adding to the different scope of earthbound locomotor techniques.

2. **Myotomal Muscles and Undulatory Movement:**
Myotomal muscles, organized in portioned blocks, are normal for fish and early tetrapods. While undulatory velocity controlled by myotomal muscles is appropriate for oceanic conditions, it went through alterations to oblige the requests of earthly development in later tetrapods.

3. **Particular Muscles for Cursorial and Saltatory Velocity:**

Cursorial (running) and saltatory (hopping) variations prompted the improvement of particular muscles. Appendages intended for cursorial velocity display strong extensor muscles for quick impetus, while saltatory transformations include muscles equipped for creating dangerous power for bouncing.

Bipedal Velocity:

1. Development of Bipedalism:
   Bipedalism, the capacity to stroll on two rear appendages, is a main quality of people and some dinosaur species. The development of bipedalism included adjustments in appendage structure, spinal bend, and pelvic life systems, prompting upgraded effectiveness in earthbound headway.
2. Upstanding Stance and Energy Effectiveness:
   The shift to an upstanding stance in bipedal life forms offers benefits in energy effectiveness. By adjusting the body along the upward pivot, bipeds lessen the energy use related with motion, taking into consideration delayed perseverance and travel over significant distances.
3. Practical Changes in Appendage Joints:

Bipedal motion required changes in appendage joints to help the body's weight and work with proficient development. Variations in the hip, knee, and lower leg joints add to the smooth coordination expected for bipedal strolling and running.
Cursorial Variations:

1. Specific Appendage Morphology:
   Cursorial variations are apparent in species adjusted for supported running. Appendage morphology in cursorial living beings frequently includes stretched appendages, decreased digit numbers, and alterations in foot structure, all equipped towards improving step length and speed.
2. Instances of Cursorial Transformations:

Instances of cursorial transformations have large amounts of the collective of animals. Cheetahs, with their smoothed out bodies and strong appendages, represent transformations for fast pursuit. Essentially, ponies grandstand cursorial proficiency with their lengthened appendages and digit decrease.
Saltatory Transformations:

1. Strong Rear Appendages for Hopping:
   Saltatory transformations include the advancement of strong rear appendages fit for creating dangerous power for hopping. These transformations are seen in different species, from frogs and kangaroos to grasshoppers, each exhibiting exceptional appendage structures for successful saltatory headway.

2. Muscle Versatility and Energy Stockpiling:

Bouncing creatures depend on muscle versatility and energy stockpiling instruments for powerful impetus. Muscles go about as springs, putting away and delivering energy during a leap, permitting life forms to accomplish great levels and distances with negligible energy consumption.
Arboreal Variations:

1. Getting a handle on Appendages and Prehensile Tails:
   Arboreal transformations are custom fitted for life in trees and incorporate appendages with particular getting a handle on capacities. Prehensile tails, tracked down in certain species, add to steadiness and mobility in arboreal conditions, permitting organic entities to explore complex covering structures.
2. Opposable Digits and Brachiation:

Opposable digits, equipped for getting a handle on objects, are normal in arboreal species. Brachiation, or arm-swinging headway, is seen in primates like gibbons, where particular appendage morphology considers productive swinging between branches.
Variations for Various Earthbound Conditions:

1. Desert Variations:
   Living beings in parched conditions have developed explicit variations for endurance, remembering effective intensity scattering and adjustments for appendage designs to limit contact with hot surfaces. Models incorporate the long legs of desert-abiding ungulates.
2. Polar Transformations:
   In polar conditions, transformations incorporate appendages with protection components to forestall heat misfortune and specific foot structures for footing on frigid surfaces. Species like polar bears exhibit variations for effective earthly headway in cruel polar circumstances.
3. Various Foot Morphologies:

Earthly conditions incorporate a scope of surfaces, prompting different foot morphologies. From the cushioned paws of huge felines for quiet following to the webbed feet of waterbirds for proficient swimming, foot variations mirror the environmental variety of earthly territories.
Developmental Meaning of Earthbound Motion:

1. Colonization of Earthly Natural surroundings:
   The development of earthly velocity assumed a critical part in the colonization of different earthbound natural surroundings. The capacity to move productively ashore opened up new environmental specialties, empowering organic entities to take advantage of assets and departure predation.
2. Hunter Prey Elements:
   Earthbound headway impacted hunter prey elements, prompting the coevolution of pursuit hunters and equivocal prey. The improvement of particular variations, like speed in hunters and nimbleness in prey, molded the complicated dance of step by step processes for surviving in earthly biological systems.
3. Expansion of Locomotor Methodologies:

Earthly conditions cultivated the broadening of locomotor systems, from the quick running of hunters to the deft moving of arboreal species. This variety adds to the environmental wealth of earthly biological systems and highlights the flexibility of life to various territories.
Difficulties and Protection Suggestions:

1. Human Effect on Earthbound Conditions:
   Human exercises, including natural surroundings annihilation and fracture, present difficulties to earthbound creatures. Protection endeavors should consider the effect of anthropogenic exercises on earthbound living spaces and the versatile techniques creatures utilize for velocity.
2. Environmental Change and Earthbound Variations:
   Environmental change represents extra difficulties for earthbound living beings, influencing temperature, precipitation examples, and natural surroundings accessibility. Species with explicit locomotor transformations might confront hardships in adjusting to quickly changing ecological circumstances.
3. Protection Procedures for Earthly Fauna:

Preservation methodologies for earthly fauna include living space insurance, rebuilding endeavors, and the production of untamed life passages. Understanding the particular locomotor transformations of species is significant for carrying out successful protection estimates that address their extraordinary natural necessities.
2.3 Constraints and Challenges in Amphibian Locomotion

Creatures of land and water, while capable in both oceanic and earthbound conditions, face remarkable imperatives and difficulties in movement. The penetrability of their skin makes them helpless to parching, requesting cautious dampness guideline. Also, the double necessities of proficient swimming and powerful earthbound development lead to splits the difference in appendage structures. Transformation represents a basic test, requiring variations for unmistakable life stages. Territory misfortune, contamination, and arising microorganisms further compromise creatures of land and water, underlining the delicacy of their environments. Exploring these limitations highlights the multifaceted equilibrium creatures of land and water should strike to make due and flourish in different environmental specialties.

Chapter 3

Reptiles: Limbs, Scales, and Diverse Environments

Reptiles, a different and old gathering of vertebrates, have effectively possessed a bunch of conditions, from parched deserts to rich rainforests. This investigation digs into the multifaceted universe of reptiles, zeroing in on the advancement of appendages and scales, and their surprising variations to different biological systems. From the rambling deserts to the transcending shades of backwoods, reptiles have explored the difficulties of shifted conditions, displaying a rich embroidery of developmental developments that have permitted them to flourish north of millions of years.

Development of Appendages in Reptiles:

1. Progress from Tetrapod Predecessors:
   The development of appendages in reptiles can be followed back to their tetrapod predecessors. While certain reptiles, similar to snakes, have lost their appendages through developmental cycles, others have fostered a different exhibit of appendage structures fit to their particular environmental specialties.

2. Rambling versus Erect Appendages:
   The appendage stance of reptiles shifts, for certain species displaying rambling appendages and others embracing an erect stance. Rambling appendages, as seen in numerous reptiles, give dependability and are appropriate for exploring complex landscapes, while erect appendages, as seen in crocodilians, add to productive strolling and support.

3. Variations for Cursorial and Arboreal Velocity:

Different reptilian genealogies have developed appendage variations for explicit methods of headway. Cursorial variations, with appendages intended for running, are found in quick species like screen reptiles, while arboreal transformations, with getting a handle on appendages and prehensile tails, are seen in tree-staying reptiles like chameleons.

Scales: Defensive Covering and Natural Transformations:

1. Epidermal Scales and Dermal Defensive layer:
   Scales, made out of keratinized epidermal tissue, act as a defensive covering for reptiles. Dermal reinforcement, found in turtles and crocodilians, comprises of hard plates covered by scales, giving an extra layer of guard against hunters.
2. Keratinization and Water Preservation:
   The keratinization of scales offers security as well as helps in water preservation. Reptiles, especially those in parched conditions, have developed scales that limit water misfortune through the skin, permitting them to flourish in living spaces where water is scant.
3. Scale Variety:

Reptiles display a different exhibit of scales, going from the smooth sizes of snakes to the fell sizes of certain reptiles. Scale examples and designs frequently have ordered importance, helping with species distinguishing proof and mirroring the natural jobs of various reptiles.

Territory Transformations:

1. Desert Transformations:
   Reptiles have effectively colonized bone-dry conditions, exhibiting momentous variations for life in deserts. Elements like proficient water preservation through particular scales, tunneling conduct, and the capacity to endure high temperatures portray desert-abiding reptiles like the famous desert iguana.
2. Amphibian Transformations:
   Amphibian reptiles, including turtles, crocodilians, and ocean snakes, have developed explicit variations for life in water. Smoothed out bodies, webbed feet, and salt organs for discharging abundance salts add to their fruitful abuse of sea-going conditions.
3. Arboreal Transformations:

Tree-abiding reptiles, like chameleons and certain snakes, exhibit transformations for life in the overhang. Prehensile tails, getting a handle on appendages, and specific scales help in climbing and exploring the mind boggling designs of trees, giving admittance to a different scope of prey and keeping away from ground-based hunters.

Conceptive Systems:

1. Oviparity, Viviparity, and Ovoviviparity:
   Reptiles utilize different conceptive systems. Oviparous species lay eggs, frequently with intense, calcified shells, giving assurance to creating incipient organisms. Viviparous species bring forth live youthful, while ovoviviparous species hold eggs inside until they are prepared to incubate, joining parts of the two systems.
2. Settling and Parental Consideration:
   Settling ways of behaving and parental consideration fluctuate among reptiles. A few animal types, similar to crocodilians and certain turtles, show elaborate settling ceremonies and give insurance to their eggs. Interestingly, numerous reptiles, like snakes, depend on the covering of eggs and insignificant parental inclusion.
3. Temperature-Subordinate Sex Assurance:

Temperature assumes a urgent part in deciding the sex of numerous reptiles during early stage improvement. This temperature-subordinate sex assurance (TSD) has huge ramifications for populace elements and is especially articulated in species like ocean turtles.

Rapacious, Herbivorous, and Omnivorous Weight control plans:

1. Transformations for Carnivory:
   Numerous reptiles are rapacious hunters, showing transformations for catching and consuming prey. Particular teeth, strong jaws, and venomous organs are normal transformations in rapacious reptiles, going from the teeth of snakes to the strong jaws of crocodilians.
2. Herbivorous Transformations:
   Herbivorous reptiles, like specific turtles and iguanas, have developed variations for benefiting from plant material. Wide, smoothed jaws, specific dentition for crushing plant matter, and maturation chambers in the gastrointestinal system are trademark highlights of herbivorous reptiles.
3. Omnivorous Ways of life:

A few reptiles, including specific turtles and screens, are omnivores, benefiting from a blend of creature and plant material. This dietary adaptability permits them to take advantage of an extensive variety of food assets, upgrading their versatility to various conditions.

Toxin and Tightening:

1. Venomous Variations:
   Venomous reptiles, like snakes and a few reptiles, have specific toxin organs and conveyance frameworks for quelling prey or dissuading hunters. Toxin sythesis fluctuates, going from neurotoxins to hemotoxins, mirroring the assorted hunting systems utilized by various species.
2. Choking in Snakes:

Constrictor snakes, similar to boas and pythons, use choking as a hunting technique. Strong curls are utilized to curb prey by confining blood stream and forestalling typical breath. This variation permits constrictors to handle prey things bigger than their heads.

Social Ways of behaving and Correspondence:

1. Territoriality and Romance Presentations:
   Reptiles show different social ways of behaving, including territoriality and romance presentations. Regional way of behaving is frequently set apart by showcases of hostility, with predominant people protecting domains for taking care of or rearing. Romance showcases include elaborate ways of behaving and visual signs to draw in mates.
2. Compound and Visual Correspondence:

Compound correspondence, through pheromones, is essential for reptiles in flagging conceptive status, stamping regions, and recognizing people. Visual signs, for example, variety changes in chameleons or throat shows in anoles, assume an essential part in correspondence inside and between species.

Cover and Mimicry:

1. Secretive Hue:
   Secretive hue, or cover, is a typical variation in reptiles for staying away from predation or improving hunting achievement. Species like leaf-followed geckos and stick bugs feature noteworthy mimicry of their environmental factors, making them almost unclear from their current circumstance.
2. Batesian and Müllerian Mimicry:

A few venomous or hurtful reptiles show Batesian mimicry, where innocuous species copy the presence of perilous ones to deflect hunters. Müllerian mimicry includes different unsafe species joining on a common advance notice shading, supporting the evasion conduct of hunters.

Natural Dangers and Protection Difficulties:

1. Living space Misfortune and Fracture:
   Reptiles face dangers from living space misfortune and fracture because of urbanization, agribusiness, and deforestation. These exercises upset essential territories, restricting assets and expanding the gamble of populace decline or eradication for some species.
2. Environmental Change and Adjusted Territories:
   Environmental change presents difficulties for reptiles, influencing temperature-subordinate sex assurance, adjusting territory accessibility, and affecting the dissemination of prey and hunters. Species with particular living space prerequisites might confront challenges adjusting to quickly changing natural circumstances.
3. Unlawful Untamed life Exchange:

The unlawful untamed life exchange represents a critical danger to numerous reptile species. Interest for outlandish pets, customary medication, and extravagance products drives the overexploitation of reptile populaces, adding to decreases in wild populaces and biological system irregular characteristics.

Research Boondocks and Protection Drives:

1. Propels in Herpetology:
   Progressing research in herpetology keeps on revealing new experiences into the science, conduct, and development of reptiles. Subatomic procedures, environmental displaying, and propels in field perception add to a more profound comprehension of reptilian variety and preservation needs.
2. Preservation Methodologies and Safeguarded Regions:
   Preservation drives for reptiles include the foundation of safeguarded regions, natural surroundings reclamation, and hostage reproducing programs. Safeguarding key living spaces and executing economical administration rehearses are basic parts of reptile preservation.
3. Local area Contribution and Training:

Local area contribution and schooling assume vital parts in reptile preservation. Neighborhood people group can add to observing and preservation endeavors, while public mindfulness crusades encourage appreciation for reptiles and their natural importance.

3.1 Terrestrial Locomotion in Reptiles

Earthbound movement in reptiles addresses an entrancing cluster of transformations and systems that have developed north of millions of years. From the rambling developments of reptiles to the jogging steps of specific snakes, reptiles have enhanced their locomotor strategies to explore different earthly conditions. This investigation dives into the development of earthbound velocity in reptiles, analyzing the physical, biomechanical, and environmental perspectives that have added to the noteworthy outcome of these vertebrates ashore.

Developmental Starting points of Earthbound Movement:

1. Change from Oceanic Precursors:
   The change from oceanic to earthbound conditions denoted a huge section in reptilian development. Early reptilian predecessors probably confronted specific tensions that leaned toward variations for development ashore, prompting the advancement of appendages and the investigation of assorted earthbound living spaces.
2. Appendages as Locomotor Variations:

Appendages, whether rambling or erect, assume a significant part in the earthbound headway of reptiles. The advancement of appendages took into consideration expanded portability, investigation of new specialties, and break from oceanic hunters. Various heredities of reptiles have displayed fluctuating appendage morphologies custom-made to their particular locomotor necessities.

Rambling and Semi-Erect Appendage Arrangements:

1. Rambling Appendage Stance:
   Numerous reptiles, especially reptiles, display a rambling appendage pose where the appendages expand outward from the body. This design gives strength, particularly in exploring lopsided landscape, and is related with a side-to-side movement during strolling or running.
2. Semi-Erect Appendage Stance:

A few reptiles, like crocodilians, embrace a semi-erect appendage pose where the appendages are situated all the more in an upward direction underneath the body. This appendage game plan is helpful for more productive velocity ashore and in water, exhibiting the versatility of reptiles to various conditions.

Biomechanics of Earthbound Movement:

1. Muscle Plan and Joint Adaptability:
   The biomechanics of earthbound movement in reptiles are impacted by the course of action of muscles and the adaptability of appendage joints. Muscles work in coordination to produce the essential powers for development, and joint adaptability considers an assorted scope of movements fit to various locomotor techniques.
2. Walk Examples:

Reptiles display different stride designs, including strolling, running, and jogging. The decision of walk relies upon elements like speed, territory, and the quick social setting. The capacity to switch between various strides exhibits the adaptability of reptilian headway.

Transformations for Particular Movement:

1. Cursorial Transformations:
   Cursorial transformations for running are seen in different reptilian ancestries. Appendages might be prolonged, and body extents altered to accomplish effective running. Models incorporate the long appendages of screen reptiles and the smoothed out assortments of specific snakes.
2. Arboreal Transformations:
   Arboreal transformations permit reptiles to explore the intricacies of tree coverings. Prehensile tails, getting a handle on appendages with particular toe cushions, and a low focus of gravity are normal transformations in tree-staying reptiles like chameleons and certain snakes.
3. Tunneling Transformations:

Reptiles that possess underground conditions have advanced specific transformations for tunneling. Appendages might be adjusted for digging, and the body shape might work with productive development through soil. Snakes like sand boas embody transformations for an underground way of life.

Bipedal Movement:

1. Bipedalism in Reptiles:
   Some reptile species, like the basilisk reptile, display bipedal

movement. Bipedalism includes the utilization of rear appendages for upstanding strolling or running, and it gives benefits concerning velocity and mobility. Bipedal reptiles feature the variety of locomotor procedures inside reptilian ancestries.

2. Bipedalism in Dinosaurs and Birds:

The development of bipedalism isn't restricted to reptiles; it is a quality common by specific dinosaur genealogies and their cutting edge relatives, birds. The progress to bipedalism in dinosaurs denoted a urgent point in the development of earthbound velocity, ultimately prompting the rise of trip in birds.

Energetics of Earthly Movement:

1. Thermoregulation and Development:
The energetics of earthly movement in reptiles are complicatedly connected to thermoregulation. Numerous reptiles are ectothermic, depending on outside heat sources to control internal heat level. Proficient motion permits reptiles to get to various warm conditions for thermoregulation.

2. Trap Predation versus Pursuit Predation:

The energy used during earthly headway is impacted by the hunting system utilized by reptiles. Trap hunters might preserve energy through covertness and unexpected eruptions of development, while pursuit hunters, like a few snakes, take part in delayed pursues to catch prey.

Natural Impacts on Earthbound Velocity:

1. Substrate and Surface Variations:
Various substrates, including sand, soil, and shakes, present interesting difficulties to earthbound velocity. Reptiles have developed transformations in appendage morphology, scales, and body shape to explore different surfaces actually. For instance, sand-abiding reptiles might have bordered scales for further developed footing.

2. Climbing and Slipping:

Climbing and slipping transformations are essential for reptiles possessing vertical surfaces or trees. Appendages with particular designs, like hooks or cement cushions, help in climbing. Snakes display one of a kind locomotor capacities, utilizing a blend of undulation and holding to climb and plummet trees.

United Development in Earthbound Velocity:

1. Comparable Answers for Comparative Difficulties:
   Merged development is obvious in the comparative arrangements that different reptilian genealogies have freely advanced to address normal locomotor difficulties. Practically equivalent to transformations, for example, appendage morphology or walk designs, mirror the particular tensions of explicit natural jobs.
2. Instances of Assembly:

Instances of assembly in reptilian velocity remember similitudes for appendage structure between remotely related species. For example, the body structure and appendage transformations of specific desert-abiding reptiles might meet with those of irrelevant species in other dry districts.

Fossorial Variations and Appendage Decrease:

1. Appendage Decrease in Snakes:
   The advancement of fossorial variations in snakes has prompted appendage decrease. While certain snakes hold minimal rear appendages, others, similar to pythons and boas, need outside appendages through and through. This appendage decrease is a transformation for tunneling and a smoothed out body structure.
2. Body Prolongation and Particular Skulls:

Fossorial transformations reach out past appendage decrease to incorporate extended bodies and concentrated skull structures. Snakes adjusted for tunneling frequently have directed noses and adaptable jaws toward work with proficient development through soil.

Future Headings in Reptilian Motion Exploration:

1. Mix of Biomechanics and Conduct:
   Future exploration in reptilian velocity ought to zero in on the coordination of biomechanics and conduct. Understanding how biomechanical transformations impact conduct methodologies will give an all encompassing point of view on the practical parts of earthly movement.
2. Effect of Natural Changes:
   The effect of natural changes, including environmental change and territory adjustment, on reptilian headway warrants examination. Exploration can investigate how shifts in temperature, substrate structure, and vegetation influence the versatile systems of reptiles.
3. Mechanical Advances in Movement Studies:

Progresses in innovation, like rapid cameras, movement examination programming, and advanced mechanics, offer new roads for concentrating on reptilian motion. These instruments can give point by point experiences into the mechanics of development, considering a more profound comprehension of locomotor transformations.

3.2 Arboreal Locomotion: Climbing and Swinging

Arboreal velocity, the craft of traveling through trees, is a particular type of earthly movement adjusted by different creatures to explore the mind boggling conditions of woods coverings. This method of development is especially noticeable in reptiles, warm blooded animals, and certain creatures of land and water. Among the horde methodologies utilized in arboreal headway, climbing and swinging are two noteworthy transformations that feature the adaptability of animals occupying tree-staying living spaces.

Climbing:

Climbing is a crucial part of arboreal motion, requiring exact coordination of appendages, specific hold structures, and a sharp comprehension of the general climate. Transformations for climbing include:

Prehensile Appendages and Tails:

Numerous arboreal creatures have appendages with transformations for getting a handle on. Prehensile hands or feet furnished with opposable digits, as found in primates, empower a solid grasp on branches. Also, prehensile tails, saw in certain reptiles and well evolved creatures, act as an extra extremity for settling and moving.

Attractions Cushions and Glue Designs:

Certain species have developed pull cushions or glue structures on their appendages, upgrading their capacity to stick to different surfaces. Tree frogs, for instance, utilize specific toe cushions that create glue powers, permitting them to climb vertical surfaces and even drop topsy turvy.

Strong Strength and Adaptability:

Climbing requires both strong strength and adaptability. Animals depending on climbing frequently areas of strength for have muscles to pull themselves up, combined with adaptability to explore through complex branch frameworks without becoming ensnared.

Swinging:

Swinging, or brachiation, is a type of arboreal velocity where animals move by swinging from one branch to another utilizing their arms. This specific technique is most quite seen in specific primates, exhibiting a novel and energy-productive approach to navigating the treetops. Key transformations for swinging include:

Long Appendages and Versatile Shoulder Joints:

Animals capable at swinging ordinarily have extended appendages, particularly the arms, which give a more drawn out reach between branches. Portable shoulder joints upgrade the scope of movement, taking into consideration a liquid and effective swinging movement.

Dynamic Arm and Hand Developments:

Swinging includes dynamic arm and hand developments, with people then again getting a handle on, delivering, and regrasping branches. This method requires outstanding coordination and strength, especially in the chest area.

Tail Variations (in Certain Species):

In specific primates, a tail adjusted for getting a handle on and adjusting helps with swinging. The tail goes about as a strengthening extremity, giving soundness during quick developments through the overhang.

Arboreal velocity, with its different systems like climbing and swinging, exhibits the striking flexibility of creatures to life in the treetops. These transformations empower productive development as well as serve basic natural jobs, permitting species to get to assets, keep away from hunters, and take advantage of the three-layered space of their arboreal territories.

3.3 Aquatic Locomotion in Reptiles

Sea-going headway in reptiles mirrors a range of variations, exhibiting their capacity to explore different oceanic conditions. While certain reptiles are completely sea-going, spending a critical part of their lives in water, others, however fundamentally earthbound, show striking swimming capacities. These variations are fundamental for exercises like scrounging, avoiding hunters, and tracking down mates. Here are key parts of oceanic motion in reptiles:

Swimming Strategies:

Reptiles utilize different swimming strategies in light of their amphibian way of life. Snakes, for instance, utilize parallel undulation, moving their bodies in a serpentine way to push through water. Crocodilians use strong parallel compasses of their tails for productive swimming, while turtles show a changed oar like appendage development.

Webbed Appendages and Straightened Tails:

Sea-going reptiles frequently include webbed appendages or leveled tails, variations that upgrade impetus through water. Webbing between the digits of turtles' appendages and the straightened tails of crocodiles add to smoothed out swimming, lessening drag and expanding mobility.

Salt Organs and Osmoregulation:

A few oceanic reptiles, similar to the ocean turtles and marine iguanas, have specific salt organs that empower them to discharge overabundance salt, working with endurance in saltwater territories. This osmoregulatory variation is essential for keeping up with the inner equilibrium of particles despite consistent openness to seawater.

Lightness Control:

Keeping up with lightness is fundamental for compelling sea-going motion. Numerous sea-going reptiles have transformations in their body structure, for example, a smoothed out shape or air-occupied spaces inside the body, which help in lightness control. Crocodiles, for example, can direct their lightness by changing the air content in their lungs.

Breath-Holding Capacities:

Sea-going reptiles have developed amazing breath-holding abilities to help delayed jumps. Ocean turtles, for instance, can stay lowered for broadened periods, depending on proficient oxygen stockpiling and diminished metabolic rates during submersion.

Thermoregulation in Sea-going Conditions:

Thermoregulation presents remarkable difficulties in sea-going conditions. Amphibian reptiles, for example, crocodiles, utilize ways of behaving like lounging on coastlines or drifting at the water's surface to direct internal heat level. The capacity to change among amphibian and earthly conditions permits them to enhance thermoregulation.

Oceanic motion in reptiles embodies the variety of versatile systems these creatures have created to flourish in water. From the twisted developments of amphibian snakes to the strong strokes of crocodiles, these transformations highlight the flexibility of reptiles in taking advantage of different biological specialties and living spaces.

3.4 Evolutionary Innovations in Reptilian Locomotion

Reptilian velocity is a demonstration of the different and creative manners by which these vertebrates have adjusted to cross the changed scenes of both earthly and sea-going conditions. More than great many years, reptiles have gone through exceptional transformative developments, prompting a range of locomotor methodologies that empower them to explore through woods, deserts, water bodies, and in the middle between. This investigation dives into the transformative developments in reptilian motion, revealing insight into the multifaceted variations that have added to their natural achievement.

Limbed Velocity: The Underpinning of Earthly Investigation:

1. Progress from Rambling to Raise Appendages:

    The development of appendages in reptiles denoted an essential progress from rambling to raise appendage stances. Early reptiles, looking like their tetrapod precursors, had appendages that spread out to the sides. Over the long run, a few heredities progressed to an erect appendage act, upgrading their capacity to walk and run productively ashore.

2. Cursorial Transformations:
   Cursorial transformations, custom fitted for running, further broadened reptilian velocity. Appendages became extended, taking into account quick development across open territory. Outstanding models incorporate the long appendages of screen reptiles, empowering them to seek after prey with speed and nimbleness.
3. Bipedal Velocity:

Bipedalism, the utilization of rear appendages for strolling or running, developed autonomously in different reptilian genealogies. Bipedal reptiles, similar to the basilisk reptile, grandstand the flexibility of appendage variations. This advancement added to sped up as well as considered productive moving in complex conditions.

Arboreal Variations: Exploring the Shade with Accuracy:

1. Prehensile Appendages and Tails:
   The advancement of prehensile appendages and tails worked with arboreal movement. Primates and certain reptiles, for example, chameleons, created appendages fit for getting a handle on branches with accuracy. Prehensile tails offer extra help, considering strength and equilibrium in the treetops.
2. Swinging and Brachiation:

Swing-like developments, or brachiation, advanced in primates and certain reptiles, including a few snakes. This imaginative type of velocity includes swinging from one branch to another utilizing stretched arms. On account of snakes, horizontal undulation mirrors the smoothness of development found in primates swinging through trees.

Amphibian Motion: Adjusting to Liquid Conditions:

1. Smoothed out Bodies and Amphibian Appendage Variations:
   Reptiles adjusted to amphibian conditions went through developmental changes to work with swimming. Smoothed out bodies, webbed appendages, and leveled tails add to effective drive through water. Ocean turtles, with their flipper-like appendages, embody the intermingling of structure and capability for marine velocity.
2. Salt Organs for Osmoregulation:
   Amphibian reptiles, especially ocean turtles, created specific salt organs for osmoregulation. These organs empower them to discharge

abundance salt, considering endurance in saltwater living spaces. This transformation is critical for keeping up with the inside equilibrium of particles despite steady openness to seawater.

3. **Lightness Control and Breath-Holding Capacities:**

Lightness control is vital to amphibian headway, and reptiles have advanced transformations to deal with their lightness. Crocodiles, for example, can direct their lightness by changing the air content in their lungs. Also, breath-holding capacities, found in ocean turtles, support delayed jumps for exercises like searching and dodging hunters.

Fossorial Advancements: Dominating Underground Movement:

1. **Appendage Decrease and Prolonged Bodies:**
   Reptiles adjusted to a fossorial way of life, staying in underground conditions, frequently show appendage decrease and stretched bodies. Limbless or diminished appendage species, like snakes, have developed a smoothed out structure that works with productive development through soil.
2. **Specific Skulls for Tunneling:**

Fossorial variations reach out past appendages to incorporate particular skull structures. Snakes, adjusted for tunneling, frequently have pointed noses and adaptable jaws, permitting them to explore through soil easily. This development exhibits the reconciliation of cranial variations with locomotor methodologies customized to underground territories.

United Advancement: Answers for Normal Difficulties:

1. **Comparable Arrangements Across Assorted Heredities:**
   United advancement is obvious in the comparative arrangements that different reptilian ancestries have freely developed to address normal locomotor difficulties. Practically equivalent to transformations, for example, appendage morphology or stride designs, mirror the particular tensions of explicit natural jobs.
2. **Instances of Combination:**

Instances of assembly in reptilian motion remember likenesses for appendage structure between remotely related species. The body structure and appendage variations of specific desert-staying reptiles might meet with those of irrelevant species in other parched locales, underscoring the versatility of reptiles to explicit conditions.

Combination of Biomechanics and Conduct: Propelling Motion Studies:

1. Mechanical Advances in Motion Studies:
   Continuous exploration in reptilian movement coordinates biomechanics with conduct. Innovative advances, like rapid cameras, movement examination programming, and mechanical technology, offer new roads for concentrating on the mechanics of development. These instruments give point by point experiences into the utilitarian parts of earthbound, arboreal, and sea-going headway.
2. Effect of Ecological Changes:

Future examination ought to investigate the effect of natural changes, including environmental change and living space modification, on reptilian movement. Exploring how shifts in temperature, substrate organization, and vegetation influence the versatile procedures of reptiles will add to a more profound comprehension of their locomotor adaptability.

Chapter 4

Birds: Wings, Flight, and Beyond

Birds, the main living relatives of the dinosaurs, have developed into a different and interesting gathering of creatures with a characterizing highlight - the capacity to fly. This exceptional transformation has molded their life systems as well as affected their way of behaving, nature, and developmental history. In this investigation, we dig into the mind boggling universe of birds, zeroing in on the complexities of their wings, the mechanics of flight, and the more extensive perspectives that go past taking off through the skies.

II. Life systems of Wings: Padded Wonders

Feathers are the trademark component of avian life systems, giving the primary establishment to flight. Isolated into shape feathers, flight feathers (remiges and rectrices), and down feathers, each type fills an unmistakable need. The mind boggling design of quills, comprising of spikes, barbules, and hooklets, guarantees streamlined proficiency as well as assumes a urgent part in thermoregulation and correspondence. The demonstration of trimming, where birds carefully keep up with their plumes, mirrors the significance of these designs in their day to day routines.

III. Skeletal Variations for Flight: Softness and Unbending nature

The skeleton of birds is a wonder of variation for flight. To accomplish the essential daintiness, avian bones are empty and melded, diminishing load without compromising strength. The fall, an augmentation of the breastbone or sternum, fills in as an anchor for the strong flight muscles. The inflexibility of the skeletal design supplements the unique idea of flight, giving the vital steadiness during ethereal moves.

IV. Muscles and Controlling Flight: Accuracy Moving

The mechanics of avian flight depend on a mind boggling exchange of muscles, especially the pectoral and supracoracoideus muscles. The pectoral muscles are answerable for the downstroke of the wing, creating the push required for lift. Interestingly, the supracoracoideus muscle works with the upstroke, finishing the recurrent wingbeat. This perplexing coordination of muscles permits birds to accomplish the accuracy and power expected for supported flight.

V. Sorts of Wings and Their Variations: Making Ethereal Works of art

The variety of bird species is reflected in their plumage as well as in the plan of their wings. Various kinds of wings have advanced to suit explicit environmental specialties and flight styles. Birds with curved wings, like sparrows and pigeons, succeed in mobility, exploring through thick conditions. Fast wings, tracked down in swifts and hawks, are intended for quick, unique flight, permitting these birds to pursue prey or dodge hunters. High-perspective proportion wings, normal for taking off birds like gooney birds and hawks, advance productivity during extremely long travel, exhibiting the flexibility of avian trip to different natural difficulties.

VI. Advancement of Flight: Disentangling the Avian Excursion

The development of trip in birds is a story set up in the fossil account and formed by the particular tensions of their surroundings. The beginning of flight can be followed back to little, padded dinosaurs that created skimming skills. After some time, these tribal structures went through versatile radiation, prompting the rise of different avian genealogies with specific flight variations. The Archaeopteryx, a momentary fossil with padded wings and dinosaurian highlights, fills in as a basic connection in understanding the steady change from land-staying dinosaurs to elevated birds.

VII. Past Flight: Avian Ways of behaving and Variations

Flight isn't just a method for transportation for birds; it includes a horde of ways of behaving and transformations that add to their endurance and conceptive achievement. Relocation, a striking accomplishment embraced by numerous species, includes extremely long travel to get to occasional assets. Romance showcases, described by intricate customs and dynamic plumage, are necessary to drawing in mates and guaranteeing effective generation. Home structure ways of behaving change broadly among species, reflecting transformations to different territories and biological specialties.

VIII. Correspondence in the Avian World: Melodies, Calls, and Visual Presentations

Birds have created perplexing correspondence frameworks that include a blend of vocalizations, visual shows, and non-verbal communication.

Warblers, like robins and songbirds, participate in intricate singing to a lay out area and draw in mates. Calls fill different needs, including cautioning of hunters, planning bunch developments, and flagging trouble. Visual showcases, frequently joined by vocalizations, assume a urgent part in romance ceremonies and building up friendly securities inside bird networks.

IX. Regenerative Systems: From Settling to Parental Consideration

The conceptive methodologies of birds are different and finely tuned to their biological jobs. Settling ways of behaving range from the perplexing woven homes of passerines to the ground homes of shorebirds. A few animal groups take part in helpful reproducing, where people past the mating pair add to raising posterity. Parental consideration includes exercises like taking care of, safeguarding, and showing juveniles, guaranteeing their endurance during the weak beginning phases of life.

X. Flightless Birds: Adjusting to Earthbound Domains

While flight is a principal quality of birds, a few animal categories have adjusted to earthbound conditions and lost the capacity to fly. Flightless birds, for example, ostriches and penguins, exhibit exceptional transformations in their life systems and conduct. Solid, cursorial legs and decreased wings are normal highlights among flightless birds, empowering them to flourish in unambiguous territories where flight offers little benefit. The development of flightlessness is a demonstration of the flexibility of birds to different environmental difficulties.

XI. Dangers to Avian Populaces: Human Effect and Protection Difficulties

In spite of their exceptional transformations, birds face various dangers in the cutting edge world, fundamentally because of human exercises. Territory misfortune, contamination, environmental change, and direct abuse present critical difficulties to avian populaces around the world. Preservation endeavors are essential to saving biodiversity, and drives like territory reclamation, hostage reproducing programs, and the foundation of safeguarded regions assume a crucial part in defending the eventual fate of birds.

4.1 Evolution of Flight in Birds

The advancement of trip in birds remains as perhaps of the most unprecedented story throughout the entire existence of life on The planet. From the taking off grandness of hawks to the quick accuracy of hummingbirds, flight has empowered birds to overcome the skies and take advantage of assorted environmental specialties. This investigation takes us on an excursion through the ages, disentangling the secrets of how birds, when grounded in the earthbound domain, developed the capacity to take off and turn into the avian wonders we witness today.

Starting points of Avian Flight

The starting points of avian flight follow back to a far off period, well before birds graced the skies. The progress from non-avian dinosaurs to genuine birds is set apart by essential transformative turns of events. Padded dinosaurs, like the Archaeopteryx, address basic momentary structures, displaying both reptilian and avian qualities. These early padded animals probably used their quills for protection, show, and possibly skimming, making way for the development of genuine flight.

Feathers: The Antecedents to Flight

The development of quills assumed an essential part in the improvement of avian flight. At first advanced for protection and show, feathers became multifunctional variations. Their lightweight design, joined with the capacity to produce lift, considered simple coasting. After some time, normal choice inclined toward adjustments in feather structure, prompting the advancement of additional streamlined structures that empowered supported flight.

Skeletal Transformations for Flight

The progress to flight required tremendous changes in the skeletal design of morning people. The advancement of lightweight and melded bones diminished by and large weight, improving the proficiency of flight. The improvement of a fall, a conspicuous edge on the breastbone, filled in as an anchor for strong flight muscles. This transformation worked with the descending stroke of the wings, vital for creating lift during flight.

Strong Elements: Fueling the Skies

The development of flight muscles assumed a significant part in empowering birds to become airborne. Avian flight muscles are metabolically serious, requiring proficient energy use for supported aeronautical movement. The separation of flight muscles, like the pectoralis and supracoracoideus, considered the many-sided coordination required for strong wing beats, prompting upgraded lift and mobility.

The Archaeopteryx: Connecting Two Universes

The Archaeopteryx, a wonderful fossil revelation, fills in as an extension between padded dinosaurs and current birds. This confounding animal had both avian and reptilian elements, including plumes and teeth. The Archaeopteryx probably participated in a type of floating or short eruptions of flight, addressing a beginning phase in the development of fueled flight.

Specific Tensions and Variations

The advancement of trip in birds was molded by particular tensions forced by the climate. The capacity to fly gave various benefits, including admittance to new food sources, escape from hunters, and effective extremely long travel. Birds that displayed even slight benefits in flight abilities were leaned toward by normal determination, prompting the refinement and streamlining of flight variations over progressive ages.

Versatile Radiation: Taking advantage of Natural Specialties

The development of flight empowered birds to go through versatile radiation, enhancing into a large number of structures to take advantage of different environmental specialties. Birds colonized assorted natural surroundings, going from open skies and thick backwoods to seagoing conditions. Each biological specialty introduced novel difficulties, prompting the development of particular transformations that upgraded trip for explicit ways of life.

Difference of Flight Styles

As birds transmitted into various conditions, their flight styles separated in light of environmental necessities. Coasting, floating, taking off, and nimble moving are only a couple of instances of the different flight styles that developed because of explicit particular tensions. Raptors, like birds and hawks, grew strong wings for taking off and exact flying hunting, while hummingbirds developed the extraordinary capacity to drift, removing nectar from blossoms with unrivaled nimbleness.

Developmental Advancements in Wing Plan

The advancement of flight is unpredictably connected to the developments in wing plan that happened more than large number of years. Various types of birds display different wing shapes and sizes, each finely tuned to their particular environmental jobs. From the long, directed wings of transitory birds toward the short, adjusted wings of timberland staying species, wing morphology mirrors the transformative variations that improve trip for explicit conditions and ways of behaving.

Significant Distance Movement: Airborne Odysseys

The advancement of flight opened up the opportunities for significant distance movement, permitting birds to take advantage of occasional assets across tremendous geological reaches. Movement is a complicated conduct formed by hereditary inclination and ecological signs. The capacity to navigate huge number of kilometers during yearly movements features the productivity and perseverance that avian flight has accomplished through developmental cycles.

Development of Flightless Birds: Exploring Earthbound Domains

While flight presented various benefits, a few birds have developed flightlessness because of explicit natural tensions. Flightless birds, for example, ostriches and penguins, show variations that enhance their earthbound ways of life. Solid, cursorial legs and diminished wings are normal elements among flightless birds, permitting them to flourish in conditions where flight offers little benefit.

Transformative Compromises: The Expenses and Advantages of Flight

The development of trip in birds accompanies inborn compromises. The physical and physiological transformations expected for flight force requirements on different parts of a bird's science. The energy requests of flight require productive respiratory and cardiovascular frameworks, and the smoothed out body shape improved for flight might restrict ground-based portability. These compromises highlight the many-sided balance between the advantages and expenses of trip in avian advancement.

Human Effect and Protection Difficulties

As human exercises keep on affecting the climate, birds face new difficulties in their battle for endurance. Living space misfortune, con-tamination, environmental change, and direct mistreatment present huge dangers to avian populaces around the world. Preservation endeavors are essential to saving the variety of bird species, and drives like environ-ment reclamation, hostage reproducing programs, and the foundation of safeguarded regions assume a crucial part in shielding the eventual fate of birds.

4.2 Wing Morphology and Aerodynamics

The class and accuracy of avian flight have enraptured human creative mind for a really long time. At the core of this authority lies the mind boggling connection between wing morphology and optimal design. Birds have developed an amazing exhibit of wing shapes and sizes, each custom fitted to their particular natural specialties and flight prerequisites. In this investigation, we dive into the captivating universe of wing morphol-ogy and streamlined features, revealing the transformative variations that empower birds to explore the skies with unmatched elegance.

1. The Material of Flight: Variety in Wing Morphology
1. Circular Wings: Accuracy in Mobility

   Circular wings are described by a somewhat short wingspan and adjusted tips, framing a curved shape when broadened. This wing morphology is appropriate for exact mobility, making it ideal for birds exploring through jumbled conditions like woods. Species like sparrows and pigeons grandstand the adequacy of circular wings, permitting them to easily shoot among branches and arrange re-stricted spaces.

2. Rapid Wings: Cutting Through the Air

   Rapid wings, interestingly, are extended with pointed tips, look-ing like a smooth, streamlined plan. This wing morphology is im-proved for quick, unique flight, working with fast developments and high velocity pursuits. Birds like hawks and swifts epitomize the effectiveness of rapid wings, empowering them to slice through the air with negligible drag and accomplish noteworthy speeds.

3. **High-Viewpoint Proportion Wings: Seasoned veterans at Taking off**

   High-viewpoint proportion wings are prolonged with a restricted harmony and a high wingspan, looking like a lengthy square shape. This wing configuration is adjusted for taking off and skimming over significant distances. Gooney birds and falcons, known for their broad maritime or aeronautical voyages, influence high-perspective proportion wings to tackle updrafts and cover huge scopes with negligible exertion.

4. **Anhedral and Dihedral Wings: Steadiness in Flight**

Wing direction likewise assumes a significant part in flight elements. Anhedral wings incline descending from the body, advancing security and dexterity. Birds with anhedral wings, like gulls, succeed in powerful, low-elevation flight, making fast changes because of changing breeze designs. Then again, dihedral wings point up, improving soundness during taking off. Raptors like falcons use dihedral wings to keep up with consistent coasts while looking over the scene for prey.

II. Streamlined features: Creating Lift and Push

1. **Producing Lift: The Way to Supported Flight**

   Lift, the power that neutralizes gravity and empowers birds to remain airborne, is a basic guideline of optimal design. The state of a bird's wing is unpredictably connected to lift age. The bended upper surface and compliment lower surface of the wing make different pneumatic forces. As wind streams all the more quickly over the bended upper surface, it makes a locale of low tension, pulling the wing up. This tension differential creates lift, permitting birds to oppose gravity and remain on high.

2. **Push and Drive: The Force of the Downstroke**

   Push, the forward force that moves a bird through the air, is produced principally during the downstroke of the wingbeat. The strong muscles associated with the breastbone drive the wings descending, making push and pushing the bird ahead. The upstroke, while adding to generally wing productivity, isn't as basic for drive. This unbalanced movement during the wingbeat cycle upgrades energy consumption and improves the effectiveness of avian flight.

3. **Wing Stacking: Adjusting Weight and Wing Region**

Wing stacking, the proportion of a bird's weight to its wing region, is a basic component impacting flight execution. Birds with lower wing stacking, where the wings support less weight per unit region, frequently display more flexibility flight. Hummingbirds, with their little weight and huge wing region, exhibit low wing stacking, permitting them to float with wonderful deftness. Alternately, birds with higher wing stacking, like falcons, succeed in taking off and covering broad distances with negligible energy consumption.

III. Transformations for Particular Flight Styles

1. Drifting: The Hummingbird's Expressive dance
   Drifting is a particular flight style showed by hummingbirds, extraordinarily adjusted to remove nectar from blossoms. The capacity to stay fixed in mid-air requires uncommon wing control and fast wingbeat frequencies. Hummingbirds accomplish this accomplishment by turning their wings in a figure-eight example, producing lift on both the upstroke and downstroke. This perplexing mobility permits them to get to nectar from blossoms with unmatched accuracy.

2. Taking off: Riding the Air Flows
   Taking off is a flight methodology utilized by birds to cover tremendous distances with negligible energy consumption. Raptors, like birds and falcons, are seasoned veterans at taking off flight. They use rising air flows, like thermals and updrafts along geographical elements, to acquire height and afterward float easily between thermals. The long, wide wings of taking off birds amplify lift, and their sharp capacity to peruse air flows permits them to explore the skies with unmatched effectiveness.

3. Airborne Aerobatic exhibition: Accuracy in Flight

Certain bird species, particularly those with curved wings, participate in perplexing airborne aerobatic exhibition. Starlings, known for their entrancing murmurations, grandstand synchronized developments and fast course adjustments. The circular wings of these birds give the deftness expected to such exact moves, permitting them to explore through thick runs with noteworthy coordination.

4.2 Diverse Flight Patterns in Birds

The huge range of bird species all over the planet grandstands a momentous variety in their plumage and environments as well as in their flight designs. From the aerobatic showcases of starlings to the taking off grandness of falcons, every species has developed extraordinary variations that take care of explicit environmental specialties and conduct needs. This investigation digs into the captivating universe of different flight designs in birds, disclosing the complexities of how these animals explore the skies with unmatched effortlessness and accuracy.

1. Taking off Dominance: The Elevated Lords of the Open Sky
1. Dynamic Soarers: Falcons and Birds of prey
   Falcons and birds of prey are famous images of taking off dominance, easily exploring the open sky with their wide wings and sharp vision. These raptors utilize dynamic taking off strategies, using rising air flows like thermals and updrafts along bluffs or uneven territory. Taking off permits them to cover broad distances while saving energy, making them productive trackers and regional patrollers. The great wingspan and dihedral wing shape add to their capacity to ride the undetectable roadways of the air.
2. Maritime Soarers: Gooney birds

Over the tremendous breadths of the vast sea, gooney birds display unrivaled authority of taking off flight. These seabirds are adjusted to use areas of strength for the over the sea surface, utilizing a mix of dynamic taking off and incline taking off. The high-perspective proportion wings of gooney birds, combined with their sharp capacity to lock onto wind angles, empower them to cover tremendous distances with insignificant exertion. Gooney birds feature the exemplification of significant distance, energy-effective flight designs.

II. Accuracy and Dexterity: Airborne Tumbling in Minimized Spaces

1. Starling Murmurations: Aggregate Coordination
   Starlings are prestigious for their amazing aeronautical presentations known as murmurations. These groups participate in facilitated, synchronized developments that make hypnotizing shapes and examples overhead. The nimbleness and accuracy shown during murmurations fill numerous needs, including hunter avoidance and correspondence inside the herd. The circular wing morphology of starlings, portrayed by a short wingspan and adjusted tips, improves their mobility, permitting them to explore through thick rushes with momentous coordination.
2. Swifts: Experts of Airborne Moves

Swifts are appropriately named for their remarkable speed and readiness in flight. These birds spend a critical part of their lives on the wing, getting bugs in mid-air. Swifts are portrayed by their slim bodies and long, cleared back wings, which add to their wonderful airborne mobility. Their flight designs incorporate mind boggling turns, turns, and quick course adjustments, permitting them to seek after and catch prey with unrivaled accuracy.

III. Floating and Fast Moves: The Specialty of Fixed Flight

1. Hummingbirds: Experts at Drifting
   Hummingbirds, with their minor size and dynamic plumage, are famous for their capacity to float in mid-air. This special flight design is made conceivable by the fast fluttering of their wings in a figure-eight example. The little size of hummingbirds, combined with low wing stacking, empowers them to create adequate lift to check gravity. Drifting is a basic transformation for getting to nectar from blossoms with accuracy, exhibiting the developmental advancement in the flight examples of these striking birds.
2. Kestrels: The Drifting Trackers

Kestrels, a kind of hawk, show a floating flight design while chasing after prey. This conduct includes the bird keeping a fixed situation in mid-air, permitting it to examine the ground for expected prey. Kestrels use their strong wings and tail to control their situation during floating, exhibiting a one of a kind variation among raptors. This floating conduct improves their capacity to find and target little warm blooded creatures or bugs on the ground.

IV. Transient Wonders: Really long Travel Across Mainlands

1. Icy Terns: Bosses of Significant Distance Movement
   Icy terns hold the record for one of the longest transitory excursions in the avian realm. These birds embrace a surprising full circle movement of north of 40,000 kilometers, going between their Cold favorable places and Antarctic taking care of regions. The flight examples of Icy terns include a mix of taking off, floating, and fluttering, permitting them to cover huge distances over seas. Their capacity to explore across mainlands mirrors the multifaceted transformations expected for significant distance, perseverance flights.
2. Sandhill Cranes: Airborne Odyssey Across North America

Sandhill cranes are eminent for their amazing transient flights, frequently covering large number of kilometers during their occasional excursions. These huge birds participate in V-development flights, an example usually connected with many relocating species. The V-arrangement fills numerous needs, including energy protection and improved correspondence inside the group. The main bird in the V makes an elevate that diminishes air opposition for the supporters, adding to the general productivity of the significant distance relocation.

V. Nighttime Guides: Flight Examples In obscurity

1. Owls: Quiet Trackers of the Evening
   Owls are nighttime trackers with flight designs adjusted to their evening exercises. These birds have particular transformations that empower them to fly quietly, critical for secretive hunting. The main edges of their wing feathers have serrations that separation the tempestuous air, diminishing commotion during flight. Moreover, the enormous surface area of owl wings, joined with a light wing stacking, considers slow and quiet flight designs, improving their capacity to shock and catch prey in obscurity.
2. Nightjars: Moths in the Evening glow

Nightjars, otherwise called goatsuckers, are crepuscular or nighttime birds with flight designs appropriate for hunting bugs in the sundown or dimness.

Their wings are adjusted for quiet flight, like owls, and they show a light-footed and sporadic flight design, catching bugs in mid-air. Nightjars are in many cases seen close to counterfeit lights, exploiting the convergence of bugs drawn to the light source during the evening.

VI. The Transformative Woven artwork of Flight Examples

The different flight designs saw in birds mirror the many-sided exchange between life systems, conduct, and natural variation. Development has woven an embroidery of flight designs, each customized to the particular difficulties and valuable open doors introduced by the climate. Whether it's the maritime dominance of gooney birds, the aggregate coordination of starling murmurations, or the quiet nighttime trips of owls, each flight design recounts an account of endurance, productivity, and variation in the powerful domain of the skies.

An Orchestra in the Skies

The skies above us are a material where birds paint an orchestra of flight designs, each stroke addressing a transformative magnum opus. From the quiet wings of owls cutting during that time to the unique soarings of birds over immense scenes, these different flight designs are a demonstration of the fantastic flexibility and strength of avian life. As we look up and observe the airborne artful dance of birds, we are helped to remember the endless innovativeness of development and the complicated associations between structure, capability, and the vast territory of the sky.

4.3 Non-flight Locomotion in Birds

Birds, famous for their dominance of the skies, are not bound to flying movement alone. While flight is a main quality, many bird species show different types of non-flight movement that assume significant parts in their day to day routines, going from scrounging and settling to keeping away from hunters and participating in romance presentations. In this investigation, we dive into the entrancing universe of non-flight movement in birds, revealing the different ways they explore earthly and amphibian conditions with exceptional versatility.

1. Earthly Motion: From Swaggering to Running
1. Strolling and Swaggering

   Strolling is a key type of earthly movement for birds. Various species have advanced particular strolling styles, frequently adjusted to their biological specialties. Swimming birds, for example, herons and cranes, display a sluggish, conscious stroll as they tail prey in shallow waters. Interestingly, ground-staying birds like chickens and quails exhibit a more fast and clamoring type of strolling. The construction of their legs and toes reflects variations for soundness and equilibrium ashore.
2. Running and Running

A few bird animal varieties have developed particular variations for fast running and running. Flightless birds, as ostriches and emus, are outstanding sprinters, equipped for arriving at great velocities. Their long, strong legs, absent any trace of quills, give effective steps, while their wings are reused for equilibrium and security. Running fills in as an essential method for dodging hunters and making progress proficiently, underlining the flexibility of non-flight motion.

II. Swimming and Oceanic Raids: Exploring Streams

1. Swimming and Rowing

   Many bird species are very much adjusted to oceanic conditions, utilizing an assortment of non-flight motion procedures to explore streams. Swimming birds, like egrets and herons, use slow, conscious strides in shallow waters while scavenging for sea-going prey. Ducks and swans, then again, participate in rowing developments, utilizing their webbed feet to push themselves through lakes and lakes. The differing variations in leg construction and foot morphology feature the variety of techniques for moving in sea-going living spaces.

2. Plunging and Submerged Drive

Certain bird species have advanced the capacity to jump and swim submerged. Penguins, for example, are momentous jumpers, involving their wings as flippers to impel themselves through the water. The variation of their wings into flippers, joined with a smoothed out body shape, works with proficient submerged development. Penguins show the way that non-flight movement can be as urgent for endurance as flight, particularly chasing prey underneath the sea surface.

III. Bouncing and Jumping: Airborne Variations Ashore

1. Bouncing as Proficient Motion
Bouncing is a typical type of earthly velocity saw in many bird species. Birds like sparrows, robins, and kangaroos utilize jumping for of proficient and quick development. The rear appendages, explicitly adjusted for strong leaps, empower birds to cover brief distances with negligible energy use. Bouncing is especially profitable in thick vegetation or lopsided territory where quick, spry developments are fundamental for searching and keeping away from hunters.

2. Jumping and Vaulting

Some bird species have advanced particular transformations for jumping and vaulting. The hoatzin, an extraordinary bird tracked down in South America, has pawed wings that guide in climbing and jumping between branches in thick tropical woodlands.

This type of headway joins parts of flightless birds' earthbound development with the spryness expected for exploring complex arboreal conditions.

IV. Romance Shows and Ritualized Developments

Non-flight headway assumes a pivotal part in romance shows and ritualized developments during the reproducing season. Birds take part in intricate moves, walks, or shows to draw in mates and lay out domain. The more noteworthy sage-grouse, for instance, performs mind boggling "swaggering" shows on customary leks, utilizing particular air sacs to make full sounds that supplement their visual exhibitions. These ritualized developments feature the significance of non-flight movement in avian social elements and conceptive achievement.

V. Settling Ways of behaving and Parental Consideration

Building homes, hatching eggs, and really focusing on youthful posterity are fundamental parts of avian life that frequently include non-flight motion. Birds take part in different settling ways of behaving, from ground homes to expand tree homes. Penguins, known for their intricate settling ceremonies, waddle ashore to gather rocks and stones to construct homes. Whenever eggs are laid, birds take part in exact developments to guarantee appropriate hatching and assurance of their posterity. Non-flight headway is basic for the outcome of these regenerative ways of behaving.

VI. Variations for Explicit Conditions

1. Cursorial Variations in Flightless Birds

   Flightless birds, for example, ostriches and emus, have advanced cursorial variations for proficient earthly movement. Their long, strong legs are appropriate for covering huge distances at high velocities. The shortfall of flight feathers diminishes generally speaking body weight, adding to improved running abilities. In these species, the development of solid, cursorial legs shows the way that non-flight movement can turn into a particular variation for endurance in unambiguous conditions.

2. Arboreal Transformations for Overhang Tenants

Birds that possess thick woodlands or tree shelters have advanced explicit variations for exploring arboreal conditions. The three-toed sloth, a bird local to Focal and South America, grandstands wonderful variations for hanging and traveling through trees. Its lengthened toes and slow, conscious developments permit it to explore treetops effortlessly. While not a bird in the customary sense, the sloth embodies the different transformations for non-flight motion in overhang staying avian species.

The Multi-faceted Universe of Avian Headway

In the complex universe of avian motion, flight is only one feature of a different collection of developments. Birds, with their mind boggling versatility, have advanced different types of non-flight movement to fulfill the needs of their surroundings, whether ashore or in water. From the accuracy of romance showcases to the proficiency of running and swimming, each type of non-flight headway adds a layer of intricacy to the complex embroidery of avian life. As we notice birds swaggering, bouncing, swimming, and participating in a heap of developments, we gain a more profound appreciation for the flexibility and resourcefulness innate in their capacity to explore the different scenes they call home.

Chapter 5

Mammals: Terrestrial, Aquatic, and Aerial Adaptations

Well evolved creatures, a different and profoundly versatile gathering of creatures, have vanquished a large number of conditions on The planet. From the taking off levels of the skies to the profundities of the seas and the immense territories of earthly scenes, warm blooded creatures feature noteworthy variations that permit them to flourish in different living spaces. This investigation digs into the entrancing universe of earthly, sea-going, and ethereal variations in vertebrates, uncovering the developmental advancements that have formed their headway, taking care of procedures, and endurance systems.

1. Earthly Variations: The Specialty of Strolling, Running, and Climbing
1. Quadrupedal Motion

   Most of earthly warm blooded creatures are quadrupeds, using four appendages for strolling and running. This essential method of motion is seen in a great many warm blooded creatures, from little rodents to enormous herbivores and hunters. The appendage construction and stride designs differ among species, reflecting variations to their natural specialties. Cursorial transformations in ungulates, like deer and pronghorn, consider quick running on open fields, while the deft developments of canids and felids are appropriate for hunting in different territories.

2. Bipedalism: An Elite Attribute

   Bipedalism, the capacity to stroll on two rear appendages, is a particular transformation tracked down in people and certain non-human vertebrates, like kangaroos and a few types of bears. The advancement of bipedalism in people has considered proficient really long travel, apparatus use, and the improvement of perplexing social designs. In kangaroos, strong rear appendages are specific for bouncing, an exceptional type of bipedal velocity that saves energy in parched conditions.

3. Climbing and Arboreal Movement

Arboreal warm blooded animals, adjusted to life in trees, show specific abilities to climb. Prehensile tails, getting a handle on hands or paws, areas of strength for and appendages are normal transformations found in tree-staying species.

Primates, like monkeys and lemurs, are adroit climbers, utilizing their getting a handle on all fours to explore through the woodland overhang. Squirrels feature lithe climbing, jumping from one branch to another, and, surprisingly, slipping trees carelessly.

4. Tunneling and Digging

A few well evolved creatures have adjusted to an underground way of life, using tunnels for safe house and insurance. Moles, for instance, have strong forelimbs and particular paws for digging through soil. They move with a trademark swimming movement, making burrows looking for bugs and night crawlers. Tunneling rodents, similar to gophers and groundhogs, display comparable transformations for a fossorial way of life.

II. Sea-going Transformations: Exploring Seas, Streams, and Wetlands

1. Pinniped Flawlessness: Seals, Ocean Lions, and Walruses

Pinnipeds, enveloping seals, ocean lions, and walruses, are very much adjusted to a semi-sea-going way of life. Their smoothed out bodies, flippers, and lard layer give proficient swimming abilities and protection in chilly waters. Seals are capable jumpers, fit for arriving at amazing profundities looking for prey. Ocean lions, with their strong forelimbs, display dexterity in both water and ashore. Walruses utilize their tusks for ice pull outs and to make breathing openings in the ice-shrouded Icy waters.

2. Cetacean Miracles: Whales, Dolphins, and Porpoises

Cetaceans, a gathering that incorporates whales, dolphins, and porpoises, are exceptionally particular for life in the oceanic domain. Smoothed out bodies, even tail accidents, and a layer of lard add to their lightness and hydrodynamic effectiveness. Dolphins, known for their insight, show gymnastic developments and productive swimming. Baleen whales, like the blue whale, are channel feeders, using baleen plates to strain little life forms from tremendous measures of water.

3. Semi-Amphibian Wonders: Beavers and Platypuses

Certain warm blooded animals have adjusted to life in both oceanic and earthbound conditions. Beavers are fantastic swimmers, involving their webbed rear feet and smoothed tails for drive. They develop elaborate dams and hotels in freshwater environments. The platypus, a monotreme found in Australia, joins elements of the two warm blooded creatures and reptiles. With webbed feet and a duck-like bill, the platypus is a gifted swimmer, scavenging for prey in waterways and streams.

III. Elevated Transformations: The Sky's the Cutoff

1. Controlled Flight: Bats and Flying Squirrels

Bats are the main vertebrates fit for supported flight. Their wings, framed from a dainty layer of skin extended between lengthened finger bones, take into consideration deft and proficient flight. Bats have adjusted to different taking care of systems, from insectivorous species that catch prey in mid-air to organic product bats that explore through thick vegetation. Flying squirrels, while false fliers, display floating variations with a patagium (a film of skin) that permits them to go between trees.

2. Taking off Levels: Stunning Aeronautical Presentations

A few warm blooded creatures have excelled at taking off through the skies. Skimming well evolved creatures, for example, colugos and flying lemurs, utilize their patagium to float between trees looking for food. While not fit for fueled flight, these arboreal lightweight flyers exhibit astounding variations for exploring complex backwoods shades. The colugo, otherwise called the flying lemur, is especially capable around evening time floating looking for products of the soil.

3. Versatile Trip in Birds and Bats

While flight is all the more regularly connected with birds, certain warm blooded animals have freely advanced flight abilities. Bats, with their altered forelimbs, are the main warm blooded creatures fit for supported flight. They assume critical parts in environments as bug hunters and pollinators. The united advancement of trip in bats and birds highlights the flexibility of well evolved creatures to assorted environmental specialties and the particular tensions that shape their developmental directions.

IV. Specific Variations for Tangible Insight

1. Echolocation: A Sonic Sensation
   Echolocation is a wonderful variation seen in certain warm blooded creatures, strikingly bats and cetaceans. Bats produce high-recurrence sound waves and utilize the reverberations to explore and find prey in complete dimness. Cetaceans, like dolphins and porpoises, use echolocation for correspondence, route, and hunting. This tactile transformation exhibits the flexibility of vertebrates in utilizing sound for spatial mindfulness and environmental communications.
2. Electroreception in Oceanic Conditions

A few vertebrates have created electroreception as a specific transformation for exploring sea-going conditions. The platypus, furnished with specific receptors in its bill, can recognize the electric fields created by the muscles and nerves of prey in the water.

This one of a kind tangible variation improves the platypus' capacity to find and catch prey, showing the different ways vertebrates have developed to communicate with their surroundings.

V. Regenerative and Parental Techniques

1. Viviparity and Parental Consideration
   Well evolved creatures are portrayed by viviparity, bringing forth live youthful, and the arrangement of parental consideration. Earthly warm blooded creatures display different regenerative techniques, from precocial species where the posterity are brought into the world in a high level state to altricial species requiring broad parental consideration. Oceanic warm blooded creatures, like dolphins and whales, additionally show viviparity and participate in complex social designs and providing care ways of behaving. Ethereal warm blooded creatures, similar to bats, have adjusted to perching ways of behaving that give security and backing to their young.
2. Exceptional Regenerative Procedures: Monotremes

Monotremes, a gathering that incorporates the platypus and echidnas, feature exceptional regenerative transformations. Monotremes lay eggs, a trademark all the more generally connected with reptiles and birds. The platypus, specifically, shows charming regenerative ways of behaving, including the creation of milk without areolas and the utilization of tunnels for settling and security.

VI. Warm Guideline and Protection

1. Fur, Plumes, and Fat
   Vertebrates have developed different components for warm guide-line, empowering them to flourish in assorted environments. Fur gives protection to earthly warm blooded creatures, catching air near the body and decreasing intensity misfortune. Oceanic warm blooded creatures, like seals and whales, have fat — a thick layer of subcutaneous fat that fills in as protection in cool waters. Feathers, basically connected with birds, likewise assume a part in warm guideline for specific well evolved creatures, like the flying squirrel.
2. Perspiring and Gasping

Earthbound vertebrates utilize systems like perspiring and gasping to direct internal heat level in hotter conditions. Perspiring, saw in people and a few primates, considers evaporative cooling. Gasping, regularly found in canids, considers the trading of intensity through the respiratory framework. These variations grandstand the physiological adaptability of vertebrates in changing in accordance with natural circumstances.

5.1 Quadrupedal Locomotion in Mammals

Quadrupedal motion, the utilization of every one of the four appendages for development, is a central and profoundly flexible method of movement saw across different mammalian species. From the strong dash of ungulates to the deft rushing of little rodents, quadrupedalism has advanced in vertebrates to suit different environmental specialties and step by step processes for surviving. This investigation digs into the complexities of quadrupedal headway, inspecting the physical variations, stride designs, and practical variety showed by warm blooded creatures across various conditions.

1. Life systems of Quadrupedal Appendages: The Structure Blocks of Development
1. Appendage Construction and Joint Variations
   The appendage construction of quadrupedal well evolved creatures is a significant determinant of their locomotor capacities. Appendages are ordinarily partitioned into portions — humerus and span/ulna in the forelimbs, femur and tibia/fibula in the hindlimbs — with joints giving adaptability and scope of movement. Transformations in joint design, for example, the ball-and-attachment joint of the shoulder and hip, empower many developments, fundamental for changed locomotor ways of behaving.
2. Variety in Foot Morphology
   The morphology of feet and digits changes fundamentally among

quadrupedal warm blooded creatures, reflecting transformations to various landscapes and ways of life. Ungulates, similar to ponies and deer, have hooves specific for quick running on open fields. Canids and felids show digitigrade velocity, strolling on their toes with prolonged metacarpals and metatarsals. Rodents, with their different ways of life, show transformations like mauled digits for digging or concentrated feet for climbing.

3. Muscle Game plans and Power Age

The course of action of muscles in quadrupedal appendages is vital for producing power and working with facilitated developments. Muscles are connected to bones through ligaments, taking into account the compression and expansion essential for appendage development. The size and strength of muscles change among species, reflecting variations to explicit locomotor requests. Strong hindlimb muscles, for instance, are fundamental for the impetus seen in jogging ungulates.

II. Step Examples: The Musical Dance of Development

1. Walk: The Consistent Speed
   Strolling is the most well-known and energy-productive stride saw in quadrupedal warm blooded animals. In a normal walk, each appendage in turn connects with the ground, giving solidness and backing. The strolling step is described by a standard musicality and is appropriate for exercises like scrounging, touching, and slow-paced development.

2. Jog: The Two-Beat Step
   The run is a quicker step that includes corner to corner sets of appendages moving together. As one forelimb and the contrary hindlimb connect with the ground all the while, there is a concise period where just two feet are in touch with the ground. The run is a proficient stride for covering moderate distances at a quicker pace and is usually found in canids like wolves and homegrown canines.

3. Pace: The Horizontal Orchestra
   Pacing includes the development of appendages on a similar side of the body as one. In contrast to the run, where appendages move askew, pacing appendages move along the side. While less energy-proficient than the jog, pacing takes into account sped up. A few enormous herbivores, for example, camels and giraffes, display pacing strides for fast headway.

4. Run: The Powerful Explosion of Speed
   The jog is a rapid walk portrayed by a suspension stage where each of

the four appendages are off the ground. This unique walk includes a succession of footfalls — initial one hindlimb, trailed by the contralateral hindlimb, and afterward the ipsilateral forelimb and contralateral forelimb. Running is a variation for quick eruptions of speed and is many times found in hunters like cheetahs and prey species like gazelles.

5. Bound: The Exquisite Jump

Bouncing is a type of headway that consolidates running with a progression of strong leaps or limits. This walk is seen in specific ungulates, like kangaroos, and is described by a strong push from the hindlimbs, trailed by a suspension stage where the two hindlimbs are off the ground. Jumping is an energy-productive methodology for covering huge distances in open conditions.

III. Variations for Various Ways of life: Nibblers, Hunters, and Scroungers

1. Cursorial Transformations in Ungulates
Ungulates, or hoofed warm blooded creatures, feature striking variations for cursorial (running) velocity. The lengthening of appendages, decrease of toes to hooves, and the improvement of a spring-like system in the appendage joints add to proficient running. Ungulates like ponies and deer are all around adjusted for quick development across open fields, where speed and deftness are pivotal for endurance.

2. Ruthless Pursuit: Speed and Secrecy
Ruthless warm blooded creatures, like huge felines and canids, show variations for both following and pursuit. Appendages are intended for eruptions of speed, with an adaptable spine considering fast turns and shifts in course. Felines, known for their snare style hunting, have retractable hooks for grasp, while canids depend on perseverance and cooperation for fruitful hunting.

3. Searching and Sharp Movement

A few vertebrates have developed locomotor transformations appropriate for rummaging and deft searching. Hyenas, with their strong appendages and effective jog, are capable scroungers, covering enormous distances looking for carcass. Deft omnivores, similar to raccoons, show flexible velocity, using climbing, running, and swimming to take advantage of an extensive variety of food sources.

IV. Difficulties and Variations in Testing Conditions

1. Desert Variations: Proficient Movement in Parched Scenes
   Warm blooded animals that possess parched conditions face difficulties like high temperatures and shortage of water. Desert-adjusted
   ungulates, similar to camels, show proficient headway with transformations for saving water and energy. The long appendages of camels
   lessen contact with hot desert sands, and their remarkable pacing
   stride takes into account energy-effective travel.
2. Snow capped Authority: Exploring Rugged Territory
   Hilly territory presents difficulties like steep slants and rough surfaces. Mountain goats exhibit transformations for getting over and
   crossing rough scenes. Their split hooves give footing, and a specific stride permits them to explore steep inclines with momentous
   nimbleness. Also, ibexes and bighorn sheep display sure-footed developments in elevated conditions.
3. Arboreal Headway: Climbing and Swinging

A few warm blooded creatures have adjusted to life in trees, requiring particular velocity for climbing and exploring arboreal conditions.
Primates, including monkeys and gibbons, show flexible abilities to climb
with prehensile hands and feet. Squirrels, with their nimble developments
and sharp paws, are adroit at climbing and jumping between branches.
V. Social Elements and Correspondence Through Motion

1. Social Preparing and Holding
   Quadrupedal motion assumes a pivotal part in friendly cooperations
   and holding among vertebrates. Social preparing, where people take
   part in common prepping, supports social bonds inside a gathering.
   This conduct frequently happens during times of rest and adds to
   the upkeep of social designs among specific warm blooded creatures,
   like primates and ungulates.
2. Regional Checking and Correspondence

Regional checking is a type of correspondence worked with by velocity. Well evolved creatures use aroma checking, scratching, and scouring
against surfaces to lay out regions and pass on data about regenerative
status. Wolves, for instance, participate in fragrance checking to depict
an area limits and speak with different individuals from the pack.
VI. Difficulties to Quadrupedal Headway: Adapting to Afflictions

1. Adapting to Predation: Cautiousness and Avoidance
   Quadrupedal vertebrates face steady dangers from hunters, requiring

transformations for cautiousness and avoidance. The capacity to distinguish hunters, for example, through sharp faculties or social alert calls, is urgent for endurance. Avoiding hunters includes fast speed increase, course adjustments, and the use of landscape highlights for cover and departure.

2. Adapting to Ecological Changes: Movement and Transformation

A few quadrupedal well evolved creatures participate in occasional movements to adapt to changes in ecological circumstances. Wildebeests in Africa, for instance, embrace significant distance relocations looking for crisp touching grounds. Relocation permits them to follow occasional examples of precipitation and access bountiful food assets, displaying the versatile adaptability of quadrupedal velocity.

5.2 Cursorial and Saltatorial Adaptations

The different universe of mammalian headway is a demonstration of the transformative developments that have permitted these animals to vanquish different conditions. Two striking variations, cursorial and saltatorial headway, exhibit the dominance of speed and jumping saw in specific warm blooded creatures. From the quick runners of open fields to the elegant leapers exploring complex scenes, these variations give exceptional answers for the difficulties of endurance and environmental specialties.

1. Cursorial Transformations: Quick Runners of Open Fields
1. Life systems and Appendage Construction
   Cursorial transformations are specific for fast running, making them especially appropriate for life in open conditions. Appendages are lengthened, with diminished toes or hooves, and joints are changed to give a spring-like system. The smoothed out body, combined with strong hindlimbs, limits air obstruction and augments impetus during quick development. Ungulates like ponies, cheetahs, and elands grandstand articulated cursorial transformations.
2. Productive Stride Examples
   The walk examples of cursorial vertebrates are intended for energy-productive and supported running. The jog, described by slanting sets of appendages moving together, is a typical walk seen in numerous cursorial species. This walk gives a harmony among speed and perseverance, permitting vertebrates to cover huge distances looking for food, water, or mates.
3. Thermoregulation in Open Conditions

Cursorial well evolved creatures frequently possess open, verdant fields where temperature guideline is essential. The extended appendages and digitigrade position (strolling on toes) of many ungulates add to warm dispersal, lessening the gamble of overheating during delayed runs. Productive cooling systems, like perspiring in ponies and gasping in canids, further upgrade their capacity to flourish in open, hot conditions.

II. Saltatorial Variations: The Craft of Jumping and Hopping

1. Life structures for Jumping

Saltatorial variations are particular for jumping and hopping, permitting warm blooded animals to explore perplexing and testing landscapes. Solid hindlimbs, described by strong muscles and prolonged bones, give the power expected to departure. The design of the hindlimbs fluctuates among saltatorial vertebrates, with variations like long ligaments and special joint setups to proficiently store and delivery energy.

2. Productive Velocity in Thick Territories

Saltatorial transformations are especially worthwhile in natural surroundings with deterrents like thick vegetation or rough scenes. Little vertebrates like kangaroos, bunnies, and wallabies influence saltatorial transformations to explore through complex conditions easily. The capacity to cover huge distances in a progression of strong jumps gives a competitive edge in dodging hunters and effectively scrounging for food.

3. Vigorous Proficiency and Protection

Jumping requires huge energy, and saltatorial vertebrates have developed transformations to moderate and advance energy use. The interesting life systems of the hindlimbs takes into consideration productive flexible backlash, limiting the energy cost related with each jump. This energy-productive type of velocity is particularly essential for little warm blooded animals that might have to cover enormous domains for taking care of or staying away from hunters.

III. Models from the Collective of animals

1. Kangaroos: Bosses of Saltatorial Velocity

Kangaroos are famous instances of saltatorial transformations in well evolved creatures. Their strong hindlimbs, stretched tails for balance, and solid tails add to proficient jumping. Kangaroos cover tremendous distances with a progression of strong jumps, arriving at noteworthy paces. This type of velocity isn't just energy-productive yet in addition permits kangaroos to move quickly through the Australian outback, where vegetation can be scanty.

2. Cheetahs: The Exemplification of Cursorial Speed

Cheetahs address the encapsulation of cursorial variations, succeeding in rapid pursuits. Their extended appendages, lightweight form, and concentrated respiratory and cardiovascular frameworks empower them to run at unimaginable rates. Cheetahs are adjusted for short eruptions of speed increase, permitting them to overwhelm prey in open scenes. The retractable hooks and non-retractable, specific grasping cushions on their feet give foothold during quick runs.

IV. Developmental Importance and Environmental Jobs

1. Versatile Advancement for Specialty Abuse
Cursorial and saltatorial variations address instances of versatile development customized to explicit biological specialties. These transformations empower vertebrates to take advantage of assorted living spaces, from open prairies to thick woodlands. The capacity to move productively and successfully in these conditions upgrades their possibilities of endurance, whether through fast pursuits or light-footed route of deterrents.

2. Natural Jobs in Environment Elements

The environmental jobs of cursorial and saltatorial vertebrates contribute essentially to biological system elements. Cursorial hunters, for instance, assume urgent parts in directing herbivore populaces, impacting vegetation, and keeping up with biological system balance. Saltatorial herbivores add to seed dispersal, molding plant networks, and supporting a scope of different creatures inside their environments.

5.3 Aquatic Locomotion: Swimming and Diving

Sea-going headway is an enrapturing part of mammalian way of behaving, displaying the different transformations that empower these animals to flourish in oceanic conditions. Whether nimbly swimming through the untamed sea or executing profound makes a plunge search of prey, vertebrates have developed exceptional systems for productive and powerful oceanic motion.

Swimming Variations: Exploring the Streams

1. Smoothed out Bodies and Appendages
Well evolved creatures adjusted to an oceanic way of life commonly highlight smoothed out bodies, decreasing drag and permitting

effective development through water. Appendages might be altered into paddle-like designs with webbed digits, like in seals and ocean lions, supporting impetus and controlling. The smoothed out plan limits obstruction, advancing swimming proficiency.

2. Tail Impetus

Numerous amphibian warm blooded animals, including dolphins and whales, depend on strong tail developments for impetus. The flat accidents of their tails are adjusted for pushing against the water, producing positive progress. The undulating movement of the tail, joined with the adaptability of the spine, takes into consideration light-footed and exact developments submerged.

Plunging Transformations: Investigating the Profundities

1. Lightness Control
   Warm blooded creatures have created components for controlling lightness, a basic part of jumping. Not at all like fish, vertebrates are not light naturally and have to deal with their situation in the water effectively. The capacity to control lightness permits them to plummet to different profundities with accuracy, preserving energy and changing their situation in the water segment.
2. Oxygen Capacity and Preservation

Plunging vertebrates have variations that upgrade their oxygen stockpiling and use during delayed jumps. The capacity to store oxygen in muscles and tissues, combined with an eased back pulse (bradycardia) and diverted blood stream to essential organs, permits them to persevere through broadened periods without reemerging. Whales, for example, can plunge to extensive profundities for taking care of, depending on these variations to explore the difficulties of the submerged climate.

Models from the Collective of animals

1. Dolphins: Nimble Swimmers and Stunt-devils
   Dolphins are famous for their amphibian ability, using smoothed out bodies and strong tails for quick swimming. Their amazing spryness permits them to explore through water with accuracy, making them adroit trackers. Dolphins are likewise known for their gymnastic shows, jumping and surfacing in dazzling ways, displaying the flexibility of their swimming variations.
2. Penguins: Bosses of Submerged Route

Penguins are very much adjusted to an existence of swimming and plunging. Their wings have advanced into flippers, giving exact control and strong impetus submerged. Penguins display noteworthy plunging capacities, for certain species arriving at profundities of a few hundred meters looking for prey. The capacity to explore submerged with such proficiency empowers penguins to flourish in their cool, amphibian natural surroundings.

5.4 Aerial Locomotion in Bats

Bats, the main vertebrates fit for supported flight, show unrivaled ethereal velocity capacities. With more than 1,400 species disseminated around the world, bats have developed different transformations that empower them to explore the skies with mind boggling accuracy and productivity. This investigation digs into the life structures, flight mechanics, echolocation, and biological meaning of bats' aeronautical headway, disentangling the insider facts of these nighttime experts of the night sky.

1. Life structures and Flight Variations
1. Wings and Skeletal Design
   Bats have an interesting wing structure that separates them from other flying creatures. Dissimilar to birds with padded wings, a bat's wing is a flimsy film of skin extended between lengthened finger bones. The fingers and arm bones make up the essential underlying components of the wing, and a meager layer, known as the patagium, interfaces the fingers and stretches out down to the hindlimbs.
2. Solid Power and Adaptability
   Trip in bats depends vigorously on the strength and adaptability of their wing muscles. The muscles liable for wing development are packed in the chest and are critical for changing wing shape, controlling wing beats, and executing complex elevated moves. The capacity to quickly change wing shape permits bats to adjust to various flight conditions, from slow drifting to quick, gymnastic flight.
3. Thumb and Wing Mobility

Bats display uncommon command over their wing and thumb developments, adding to their readiness in flight. The thumb, which upholds the main edge of the wing, is profoundly portable and takes into account multifaceted changes during flight. This thumb portability upgrades the bats' capacity to execute exact moves, fundamental for exploring complex conditions and catching prey on the wing.

II. Flight Mechanics: Controlled and Floating Flight

1. Controlled Flight

Bats are strong fliers equipped for maintained, controlled flight. Dissimilar to some floating well evolved creatures, bats effectively produce lift and impetus through wing fluttering. The downstroke of the wing beat gives the push expected to positive progress, while the upstroke limits opposition. The wing morphology, combined with strong flight muscles, empowers bats to cover huge distances looking for food and reasonable perching destinations.

2. Floating and Mobility

While bats are principally controlled fliers, a few animal types integrate skimming into their flight collection. Skimming is many times seen during scrounging, where bats utilize the vertical air flows close to vegetation to proficiently cover removes more. The capacity to flawlessly change between controlled flight and skimming improves their general mobility and adds to their progress in assorted living spaces.

III. Echolocation: Exploring the Dim

1. The Development of Echolocation

One of the most striking elements of bat elevated headway is their dependence on echolocation. Echolocation is a tangible variation that permits bats to explore and find prey in complete dimness by discharging high-recurrence sound waves and deciphering the reverberations that return quickly. This transformation has developed freely in different bat heredities, bringing about a variety of echolocation procedures and frequencies.

2. Echolocation Calls and Recurrence Tweak

Bats emanate ultrasonic calls, frequently past the scope of human hearing, to explore their environmental elements. The recurrence and example of these calls shift among species, reflecting variations to various scavenging methodologies. A few bats utilize steady recurrence calls, while others utilize recurrence balanced calls, changing the pitch during the call to get itemized data about their current circumstance.

3. Prey Recognition and Hunting Procedures

Echolocation is a vital device for bats in identifying and catching prey mid-air. By breaking down the returning reverberations, bats can recognize the distance, size, shape, and, surprisingly, the surface of articles in their environmental elements. This complex sonar framework permits them to find minuscule bugs with noteworthy precision, adding to their prosperity as nighttime trackers.

IV. Natural Importance and Transformations

1. Nighttime Specialty and Insectivorous Way of life
Bats have effectively involved the nighttime specialty, exploiting the wealth of flying bugs during the evening. Their insectivorous way of life has molded their variations for coordinated flight and exact echolocation, permitting them to take advantage of a huge range of biological specialties, from thick timberlands to open prairies.

2. Relocation and Really long Travel
Some bat species participate in exceptional significant distance relocations, covering hundreds or even a great many kilometers looking for occasional assets. These movements feature the perseverance and navigational abilities of bats, exhibiting their capacity to cross assorted scenes and adjust to changing ecological circumstances.

3. Perching and Hibernation

Bats display explicit transformations connected with perching and hibernation. During the day, bats perch in different protected areas, going from caverns and tree hollows to man-made structures. Their capacity to hang topsy turvy while perching is worked with by particular ligaments that secure their toes. Hibernation is one more variation that permits some bat species to endure cruel winter conditions by entering a condition of lethargy, rationing energy until good circumstances return.

V. Preservation and Dangers

1. Natural Administrations and Fertilization
Bats offer priceless natural types of assistance, including fertilization and seed dispersal. Many bat species are key pollinators for various plant species, adding to the regenerative progress of plants and the upkeep of biodiversity.
The dispersal of seeds by bats likewise assumes a vital part in environment elements, adding to backwoods recovery and plant variety.

2. Dangers and Preservation Difficulties

Notwithstanding their environmental importance, bats face various dangers, including territory misfortune, environmental change, and the spread of infections like white-nose disorder. The protection of bat populaces is significant for the soundness of environments as well as for horticultural efficiency, as bats assume a crucial part in controlling bug populaces that can be hurtful to crops.

Chapter 6

Comparative Analysis: Patterns and Convergences

The variety of creature life on Earth is reflected not just in the bunch species that occupy various environments yet in addition in the wide exhibit of velocity methodologies they utilize. From the quick trip of birds to the spry swimming of fish and the earthbound moves of well evolved creatures, the set of all animals features a surprising scope of development designs. A near examination of these velocity designs uncovers both exceptional transformations intended for specific gatherings and interesting combinations where indirectly related species have developed comparative answers for comparable difficulties. This investigation digs into the examples and combinations saw in creature headway, revealing insight into the entrancing transformations that have arisen through developmental cycles across assorted taxa.

1. Transformative Setting: Disparity and Union
1. Phylogenetic Variety and Transformation
   The transformative tree of life is portrayed by both difference and combination, where species adjust to their particular surroundings and natural specialties. While firmly related species might share normal progenitors, remotely related species may freely develop comparative qualities because of particular tensions and ecological requirements. Headway, an essential part of creature conduct, gives a focal point through which to investigate the developmental cycles that have molded the development examples of different life forms.
2. Versatile Radiation and Environmental Specialties

Versatile radiation, the fast broadening of a typical predecessor into various structures, frequently prompts the control of various environmental specialties. This cycle brings about the advancement of particular headway designs custom-made to the particular requests of different conditions. Looking at the movement of species inside the setting of versatile radiation gives bits of knowledge into the connections among structure and capability in the normal world.

II. Earthly Velocity: Appendages and Steps

1. Quadrupedal Movement
   Quadrupedalism, the utilization of each of the four appendages for development, has autonomously advanced in different gatherings, exhibiting both combination and disparity. Vertebrates like ponies and canines display cursorial variations for productive running, while reptiles like reptiles and turtles exhibit different appendage morphologies for earthbound motion. Noticing the assorted walks, from the bouncing of kangaroos to the jog of ponies, features the flexibility of quadrupedal velocity in adjusting to various biological specialties.
2. Bipedalism: Union in Upstanding Motion

Bipedal motion, the utilization of two appendages for development, has autonomously arisen in particular transformative ancestries, with birds, people, and certain dinosaurs displaying focalized variations for upstanding strolling. While the skeletal designs might vary, the utilitarian combination in the reception of bipedalism mirrors the benefits of this type of velocity in exploring explicit conditions and getting to assets.

III. Oceanic Headway: Blades, Flippers, and Tails

1. Fish: Blades and Proficient Swimming
   Fish, addressing a different gathering of sea-going vertebrates, show an assortment of blade morphologies adjusted to various swimming styles. The merged advancement of dorsal, pectoral, pelvic, and butt-centric blades in different fish species features the utilitarian meaning of these designs in accomplishing solidness, mobility, and effective impetus through water.
2. Marine Warm blooded animals: Concurrent Transformations for Oceanic Life

Marine warm blooded animals, including whales, dolphins, and seals, have concurrently advanced smoothed out bodies, flippers, and tails for productive swimming. While their nearest earthly family members are warm blooded creatures, the transformations for oceanic life exhibit hitting unions with fish. The advancement of flippers in dolphins, for instance, reflects the practical job of pectoral blades in fish, underlining the specific tensions of amphibian conditions.

IV. Aeronautical Headway: Wings and Flight

1. Birds: Various Transformations for Flight
   Birds, the essential pilots in the animals of the world collectively, show an exceptional variety of wing shapes and flight styles. From the taking off wings of hawks to the dexterous moves of hummingbirds, avian flight addresses both union and dissimilarity. The joined advancement of wings as variations for fueled flight highlights the benefits of this motion methodology in getting to assets and keeping away from hunters.
2. Bats: Mammalian Flight Merged with Birds

Bats, the main warm blooded creatures fit for supported flight, have concurrently advanced flight transformations with birds, notwithstanding their far off developmental relationship. The wing structure, fueled flight, and echolocation capacities of bats grandstand astounding combinations with avian flight, outlining the versatile worth of trip in exploring complex conditions and getting to different natural specialties.

V. Developmental Advances: From Water to Land

1. Creatures of land and water: Appendage Variations for Double Velocity
   Creatures of land and water, addressing a temporary gathering among sea-going and earthly conditions, feature appendage transformations that empower both swimming and strolling. The focalized advancement of appendages in creatures of land and water and certain fish features the transformative change from blades to appendages, permitting these life forms to take advantage of both sea-going and earthly environments.
2. Reptiles: Various Headway Techniques

Reptiles, including reptiles, snakes, and crocodilians, display different motion systems adjusted to their individual surroundings. Limbless snakes and legless reptiles feature united variations for appendage decrease, empowering effective development in restricted spaces. The combination of stretched bodies and sidelong undulation in snakes and legless reptiles reflects variations for effective earthly velocity.

VI. Developmental Advancements: From Ground to Sky

1. Arboreal Movement: Climbing and Swinging
   Arboreal headway, the development inside trees, has freely advanced in different gatherings, displaying united transformations for climbing and swinging. Primates, like monkeys and gibbons, display prehensile hands and feet for getting a handle on branches, while irrelevant vertebrates like squirrels and reptiles like chameleons grandstand comparable transformations for exploring arboreal conditions.
2. Skimming: Assemblies in Airborne Development

Coasting, the controlled plunge from a level, has concurrently developed in different taxa. Flying squirrels, coasting lemurs, and floating reptiles like flying mythical serpents grandstand different morphological transformations for accomplishing controlled skims. While the heredities are unmistakable, the combination in skimming transformations stresses the particular benefits of this motion procedure in getting to assets and staying away from ground-based hunters.

VII. Transformative Examples in Outrageous Conditions

1. Desert Variations: Appendage Morphology and Thermoregulation
   Desert-staying species, going from well evolved creatures to reptiles, show united transformations for productive headway in bone-dry conditions. Cursorial variations, like extended appendages for quick running, have freely advanced in desert-abiding warm blooded animals like kangaroos and reptiles like the screen reptile. Moreover, focalized transformations for thermoregulation, like intelligent scales in specific reptiles, feature the difficulties of outrageous conditions.
2. Polar Variations: Assembly in Cool Conditions

Species occupying polar areas, like the Icy and Antarctic, grandstand merged transformations for movement in cool conditions. The smoothed out bodies and flipper-like appendages of marine warm blooded animals like seals and penguins feature combinations in accomplishing productive swimming and making a plunge frigid waters. Also, the protection given by thick fur or lard reflects joined transformations for thermoregulation in chilly environments.

VIII. Imperatives and Difficulties: The Constraints of Velocity

1. Requirements on Size: Scaling Regulations and Transformations
   The size of a life form forces imperatives on its motion capacities, as apparent in the scaling regulations that administer the connection between body size and metabolic rates. Huge creatures face difficulties connected with energy use and intensity dissemination, prompting merged transformations like productive strides and concentrated respiratory frameworks. Then again, little creatures might experience imperatives connected with keeping up with steadiness and producing adequate power for compelling headway.
2. Ecological Difficulties: Adapting to Changed Natural surroundings

Creatures should explore assorted environments, each introducing extraordinary difficulties to movement. Joined transformations for proficient development across various landscapes, for example, sand-swimming variations in reptiles and particular appendage morphology in cursorial warm blooded animals, feature the adaptability of movement systems in beating ecological difficulties.

6.1 Shared Principles in Vertebrate Locomotion

The different cluster of vertebrate life on Earth incorporates species occupying earthbound, sea-going, and aeronautical conditions, each exhibiting astounding variations for motion. Notwithstanding the clear distinctions in structure and capability among vertebrates, a nearer assessment uncovers shared rules that highlight the solidarity of their developmental legacy.

This investigation dives into the ongoing ideas woven into the embroidered artwork of vertebrate movement, unwinding the basic rules that have arisen across particular heredities and conditions.

1. Skeletal Engineering: The Groundwork of Development
1. Appendage Morphology and Capability
   The skeletal design of vertebrates assumes a critical part in characterizing their methods of velocity. Appendage morphology fluctuates broadly, reflecting transformations to explicit conditions and ways of life. From the rambling appendages of reptiles to the cursorial transformations in warm blooded creatures and the smoothed out balances of fish, the variety of appendage structures covers hidden likenesses in the key standards of skeletal help, joint enunciation, and solid connection.
2. Kinematic Requirements and Step Examples

In spite of the variety in appendage morphology, vertebrates frequently display shared kinematic imperatives and step designs. Quadrupedal warm blooded animals, for example, usually utilize even steps like the jog, while bipedal species embrace uneven strides like strolling or running. The assembly in stride designs uncovers the impact of biomechanical rules that upgrade energy effectiveness, solidness, and mobility across various vertebrate heredities.

II. Solid Elements: From Compression to Coordination

1. Muscle Withdrawal and Power Age
   Muscles act as the motors of vertebrate velocity, producing the power expected for development. The standards of muscle withdrawal, controlled by the biochemical cycles of actin and myosin collaboration, are shared across vertebrate taxa. Whether it's the strong fluttering of bird wings, the undulating movement of fish blades, or the synchronized steps of running vertebrates, the key standards of muscle elements add to the variety of headway techniques.
2. Facilitated Development and Neuromuscular Control

Facilitated development includes the mix of tangible information, brain handling, and exact neuromuscular control. Vertebrates share normal standards of brain association that empower facilitated and versatile reactions to natural improvements during movement. From the perplexing brain circuits organizing appendage developments in warm blooded creatures to the calibrated changes of wing beats in birds, the basic standards of neuromuscular control uncover the transformative resourcefulness of vertebrate movement.

III. Energetics: Adjusting the Books of Headway

1. Metabolic Use and Productivity
   Energetics assume an essential part in vertebrate headway, impacting the metabolic use expected for development. The standards of metabolic productivity are divided between vertebrates, with variations customized to upgrade energy use in view of biological requests. Cursorial well evolved creatures, for instance, display variations for effective rushing to cover huge distances, while ethereal species, for example, birds and bats, balance energy utilization during trip through changed wing morphologies and flight styles.
2. Thermoregulation and Energy Protection

Thermoregulation is complicatedly connected to motion, particularly in deciding when and how creatures move to improve energy preservation. Whether it's the luxuriating conduct of reptiles to ingest sun based heat or the gasping of vertebrates to disperse abundance heat during effort, the common standards of thermoregulation highlight the significance of keeping an ideal energy balance for supported motion.

IV. Tangible Coordination: Exploring the Climate

1. Vision and Spatial Mindfulness

   Vision assumes a urgent part in vertebrate motion, offering pivotal data for exploring the climate and keeping away from obstructions. The standards of visual insight are shared across vertebrates, with variations mirroring the particular natural specialties and movement systems of various species. From the sharp vision of birds for flying route to the binocular vision of hunters for profundity insight, the standards of visual data handling add to the outcome of different motion modes.

2. Proprioception and Sensation Mindfulness

Proprioception, the familiarity with body position and development, is major to vertebrate motion. Shared standards of proprioceptive criticism permit creatures to keep up with balance, execute exact developments, and adjust to changes in landscape. The complexities of appendage arrangement in earthbound warm blooded animals, the hydrodynamic changes in swimming fish, and the mid-air aerobatic exhibition of flying bats all depend on the standards of proprioception for viable movement.

V. Ecological Collaborations: Headway in Setting

1. Transformations to Landscape and Substrate

   The standards of headway stretch out past the biomechanics of the creature to envelop cooperations with explicit landscapes and sub-strates. Whether crossing rough scenes, sandy deserts, or oceanic conditions, vertebrates show shared transformations in appendage morphology, walk examples, and body stance to enhance develop-ment in light of ecological difficulties. These transformations mirror the common standards of movement inside the setting of different environments.

2. Lightness and Hydrodynamics

Sea-going vertebrates, including fish, marine warm blooded animals, and creatures of land and water, stick to shared standards of lightness and hydrodynamics for productive movement in water. Variations like swim bladders in fish, smoothed out bodies in marine vertebrates, and webbed feet in creatures of land and water all embody the joined advancement of designs intended to limit drag and amplify drive, mirroring the common standards of movement in amphibian conditions.

VI. Combination in Outrageous Conditions

1. Outrageous Conditions: Difficulties and Arrangements
   Vertebrates occupying outrageous conditions, like deserts, polar lo-cales, and high heights, display concurrent variations that rise above ordered limits. The standards of movement in these conditions include conquering difficulties connected with temperature limits, low oxygen levels, and concentrated assets. Focalized variations, for example, the extended legs of desert-staying vertebrates or the pro-tecting fur of polar bears, show the common standards of movement in outrageous circumstances.

2. Combination in Flight: Birds and Bats

Flight, a perplexing type of motion, exhibits exceptional union among birds and bats, in spite of their developmental difference. The standards of optimal design, wing morphology, and energy-effective flight designs uncover shared techniques for exploring the flying domain. Whether it's the fluttering wings of birds or the adaptable film wings of bats, the stan-dards of lift, push, and mobility are united answers for the difficulties of three-layered aeronautical motion.

VII. Developmental Advances: Disentangling the Strings of Progress

1. Changes between Motion Modes
   The developmental changes between various movement modes, for example, shifts from oceanic to earthly or from strolling to flying, uncover shared rules that rise above phylogenetic limits. The trans-formations expected for these advances frequently include adjust-ments to appendage morphology, tactile organs, and energetics. Understanding the common standards hidden these changes gives bits of knowledge into the adaptability and flexibility of vertebrate movement.

2. Transformative Advancements in Arboreal Movement

Arboreal headway, the development inside trees, has freely advanced in different gatherings, including primates, squirrels, and reptiles. Shared standards of appendage prehensility, getting a handle on transformations, and tail usage reflect merged answers for the difficulties of exploring complex arboreal conditions. The development of opposable thumbs in primates and prehensile tails in specific reptiles represents the assembly in arboreal velocity methodologies.

6.2Convergent Evolution in Locomotor Adaptations

Joined development is a captivating peculiarity where indirectly related species freely develop comparative qualities or transformations to adapt to tantamount natural difficulties. No place is this more apparent than in locomotor variations across assorted taxa. Through merged advancement, various species confronting similar to environmental requests have shown up at closely resembling arrangements, displaying the brilliant manners by which nature enhances development inside unambiguous territories.

1. Cursorial Variations: The Requirement for Speed

   The quest for speed and effective running has prompted striking unions in cursorial transformations among earthbound vertebrates. Whether it's the long legs of ostriches in Africa, the strong rear appendages of kangaroos in Australia, or the smooth groups of cheetahs in Asia and Africa, these species share normal attributes notwithstanding their developmental uniqueness. The particular tensions of open natural surroundings have leaned toward variations like prolonged appendages, specific muscular build, and smoothed out bodies, underscoring the merged development of cursorial movement.

2. Skimming Authority: Focalized Transformations in Arboreal Conditions

   The capacity to skim through the woodland covering has freely developed in different gatherings, displaying focalized transformations for arboreal movement. Flying squirrels in North America, colugos in Southeast Asia, and sugar lightweight planes in Australia have all evolved patagia - films that permit them to coast between trees. In spite of contrasts in transformative genealogy, these species share a typical need to explore three-layered spaces, prompting the merged development of coasting variations.

3. Balances, Flippers, and Smoothed out Bodies: Oceanic Assemblies

   The sea-going domain has seen various cases of focalized development in locomotor transformations. Fish, marine warm blooded creatures, and reptiles have autonomously developed smoothed out bodies, balances, and flippers to move effectively through water. Dolphins and sharks, for instance, show united development in their fusiform bodies and dorsal balances, advancing hydrodynamics for quick swimming. Also, the concurrent advancement of flippers in marine well evolved creatures and ocean turtles reflects variations to the difficulties of life in sea-going conditions.

4. Suspensory Movement: Swinging from the Trees

The capacity to suspend and swing through the trees has advanced concurrently in various mammalian heredities. While primates like gibbons in Asia have created brachiation - swinging from one branch to another utilizing their arms - comparable variations are seen in specific marsupials, like tree kangaroos in Australia and New Guinea. The union in appendage morphology and conduct features the common difficulties of exploring complex arboreal conditions.

5. Elevated Authority: Birds and Bats in Flight

Flight, a complex and vivaciously requesting type of headway, has concurrently developed in birds and bats notwithstanding their unmistakable transformative chronicles. The standards of optimal design, wing morphology, and the requirement for lift and push have prompted wonderful likenesses in their variations for aeronautical movement. Whether it's the wings of falcons or the adaptable layers of bats, these united transformations highlight the upsides of trip in getting to assets, keeping away from hunters, and exploring huge domains.

6. Appendage Decrease: Assemblies in Earthbound Conditions

Appendage decrease has autonomously advanced in various heredities confronting comparative difficulties connected with motion in bound spaces. Snakes, legless reptiles, and certain well evolved creatures like the fossorial mole display concurrent variations with appendage decrease, empowering productive development in underground conditions. The common need to explore restricted spaces has prompted the advancement of prolonged bodies and concentrated methods of limbless motion.

6.3 Trade-offs and Constraints Across Taxa

The variety of life on Earth has emerged through the course of development, chiseling a huge range of structures and works improved for endurance and propagation. In the domain of motion, organic entities have developed different transformations to explore their surroundings and satisfy natural jobs.

Notwithstanding, the streamlining of one quality frequently comes at the expense of another, prompting compromises and imperatives that shape the direction of development. This investigation dives into the many-sided trap of compromises and limitations across taxa, disentangling the complicated exchange between structure, capability, and the particular tensions that oversee motion in the animals of the world collectively.

1. Lively Compromises: Adjusting the Books of Headway
1. The Expense of Speed
   The mission for speed in headway frequently accompanies critical vigorous expenses. In earthbound well evolved creatures, for example, accomplishing high paces during running requires significant energy consumption. Cheetahs, known for their wonderful speed increase and speed, experience compromises in perseverance, as running at maximum velocities rapidly exhausts energy holds. This compromise is a consequence of the requirement for strong explosions of energy to catch prey, offset the limit of supported action.
2. Perseverance in Oceanic Conditions

Sea-going conditions present an alternate arrangement of vigorous compromises. While fish, with their smoothed out bodies and blades, succeed at productive cruising through water, the persistent undulating movement expected for swimming requests a steady consumption of energy. The harmony between the requirement for supported development and energy protection shapes the advancement of fish movement, featuring the compromises inborn in exploring sea-going conditions.

II. Morphological Compromises: The State of Movement

1. Appendage Morphology in Earthly Transformations
   The morphology of appendages assumes an essential part in earthly motion, and compromises arise in the streamlining of appendage structures for different capabilities. Cursorial transformations, found in creatures like ponies and cheetahs, include appendage prolongation for effective running. Notwithstanding, this might come to the detriment of mobility and the capacity to explore thick vegetation. The compromise among speed and nimbleness is a repetitive topic in the development of appendage morphology among earthbound species.
2. Wing Morphology in Flying Transformations

In the flying domain, the shape and size of wings are basic determinants of flight execution. Birds and bats, both fit for supported flight, exhibit different wing morphologies enhanced for their particular necessities.

Birds, with their padded wings, focus on lift and mobility, while bats, with their membranous wings, center around spryness and exact control.

These distinctions in wing morphology address compromises directed by the specific tensions of their particular flight systems.

III. Tactile Compromises: Exploring Conditions with Restricted Data

1. Vision and Hear-able Awareness
Tactile transformations in headway include compromises that balance the benefits of one sense against the limits of another. For instance, hunters depending on intense vision for hunting might confront compromises with regards to hear-able responsiveness. This compromise is clear in species like owls, which have extraordinary vision however penance some level of hear-able sharpness contrasted with different birds. The streamlining of tangible abilities mirrors the natural requests of explicit locomotor techniques.
2. Echolocation and Lively Expenses

Echolocation, a wonderful variation in specific bats and marine warm blooded creatures, considers route and prey location through sound waves. In any case, this refined tactile capacity accompanies lively expenses. The creation and gathering of high-recurrence calls request significant metabolic assets, and species depending on echolocation should cautiously adjust the advantages of this tangible variation against the fiery compromises related with its utilization.

IV. Natural Limitations: Adjusting to Fluctuated Territories

1. Arboreal Difficulties
Exploring arboreal conditions presents explicit difficulties that shape locomotor variations. Species abiding in trees, for example, primates and squirrels, face compromises connected with appendage morphology and body size. While prehensile appendages give benefits in climbing and swinging, bigger body size might impede nimbleness in the shade. The compromises between appendage morphology and body size mirror the contending requests of arboreal movement.
2. Desert Difficulties

Desert conditions force imperatives on movement, affecting appendage morphology and intensity scattering systems. Cursorial transformations in desert-staying well evolved creatures, similar to the long legs of kangaroos or the smoothed out collections of sand gazelles, upgrade heat dispersal and lessen ground contact. Notwithstanding, these transformations might compromise against mobility, stressing the requirements forced by the cruel states of bone-dry scenes.

V. Regenerative Compromises: Adjusting Movement and Parental Venture

1. Regenerative Expenses of Flight
   In species equipped for flight, the requests of propagation acquaint compromises related with energy portion. For transient birds, the energy exhausted during significant distance flights might restrict the assets accessible for propagation. This regenerative compromise is clear in the relocation examples of birds, where the need to cover tremendous distances clashes with the energy prerequisites of rearing and raising posterity.
2. Parental Venture and Locomotion*

The degree of parental interest in posterity can impact locomotor variations. Species with broad parental consideration, like vertebrates with delayed times of nursing and assurance, may confront compromises concerning locomotor productivity. The obligation to parental obligations compels the significant investment accessible for scavenging and velocity, molding the development of transformations that offset regenerative accomplishment with the difficulties of development.

VI. Compromises in Outrageous Conditions: Adapting to Nature's Limits

1. Polar Transformations: Portability in Cool Circumstances
   Species possessing polar districts face novel difficulties connected with movement in chilly conditions. Compromises in protection and versatility are apparent in the transformations of polar bears and seals. While thick fur and fat give protection against the chilly, they might prevent readiness and speed. These compromises mirror the imperatives forced by the outrageous states of polar natural surroundings.
2. High-Height Difficulties

High-height conditions present limitations on oxygen accessibility, affecting locomotor variations in species staying in hilly locales. Creatures like snow panthers and mountain goats display compromises regarding respiratory effectiveness and mobility. The test of oxygenation at high elevations requires variations in respiratory frameworks that might think twice about parts of locomotor execution.

Chapter 7

Technological Insights and Biomimicry

The convergence of innovation and science has led to a field known as biomimicry, where specialists and researchers draw motivation from the regular world to take care of perplexing issues and plan imaginative arrangements. Nature, through huge number of long stretches of development, has sharpened proficiency, manageability, and flexibility in its manifestations. This investigation dives into the domain of mechanical experiences got from biomimicry, unwinding how the standards of nature have enlivened state of the art headways across different enterprises.

1. Biomimicry Establishments: Gaining from Nature's Diagrams
1. Primary Designing: Examples from the Regular Manufacturers
   Nature's draftsmen, from bugs to birds, have motivated forward leaps in underlying designing. Bug silk, known for its solidarity and flexibility, has been emulated in the production of engineered materials for applications going from tactical armor carriers to careful stitches. Essentially, the lightweight yet solid construction of bird bones has impacted the plan of airplane parts, prompting more effective and strong designs.
2. Velcro and Nature's Snare and-Circle Systems

The creation of Velcro, a universal securing framework, was motivated by the snare and-circle component saw in burrs gripping to dress. Swiss specialist George de Mestral perceived the productivity of this normal connection and made an interpretation of it into the plan of Velcro. This biomimetic arrangement has found applications in enterprises going from design to aviation.

II. Reasonable Energy Arrangements: Nature's Power Plants

1. Bio-Enlivened Sun powered Energy Catch
   Plants, through photosynthesis, effectively convert daylight into energy. Biomimicry plays had an impact in creating sun powered chargers propelled by the designs of leaves, enhancing light retention and energy transformation. This approach upgrades the effectiveness of sun based innovation as well as adds to the maintainability of sustainable power arrangements.
2. Wind Turbines and Avian Proficiency

The plan of wind turbines has been impacted by the streamlined productivity saw in avian flight. Biomimicry has prompted advancements, for example, turbine sharp edges demonstrated after the smoothed out states of bird wings. By imitating nature's plans, engineers expect to work on the exhibition and supportability of wind energy innovation.

III. Transportation Transformation: Nature's Productive Movers

1. Shot Trains and the Kingfisher's Snout
   The streamlined productivity of the kingfisher's snout, intended for smooth passage into water, has propelled the state of Japan's Shinkansen, or slug train. By imitating this regular plan, engineers have decreased commotion and opposition, prompting quicker and more effective train travel. This biomimetic application grandstands how nature's answers can improve transportation frameworks.
2. Swarm Advanced mechanics: Nature's Cooperative People group

Noticing the aggregate way of behaving of social bugs like subterranean insects and honey bees has motivated the improvement of multitude mechanical technology. These frameworks, comprising of various independent specialists working cooperatively, draw bits of knowledge from nature's productive and facilitated bunch ways of behaving. Applications range from search and salvage missions to natural checking.

IV. High level Materials: Nature's Brilliant Structures

1. Gecko-Enlivened Glues
   The gecko's capacity to grip to vertical surfaces and move easily on roofs has motivated the making of manufactured cements. Emulating the construction of gecko footpads, engineers have created materials with high cement strength yet simple delivery, tracking down

applications in mechanical technology, clinical gadgets, and even space investigation.

2. Bio-Roused Polymers and Self-Mending Materials

Nature's capacity to recover and mend has impacted the advancement of self-recuperating materials. From polymers that mirror the properties of mussel cements to materials that can fix themselves after harm, these advancements draw motivation from the regenerative abilities saw in living organic entities. Such biomimetic materials have applications in ventures going from development to hardware.

V. Advanced mechanics and Bionics: Imitating Nature's Developments

1. Mechanical Appendages and Exoskeletons
   Bionics, the mix of science and innovation, has prompted headways in prosthetics and exoskeletons. By contemplating the biomechanics of human and creature developments, engineers have created automated appendages that recreate regular usefulness. Exoskeletons, roused by the outer muscle framework, give improved strength and backing to human clients in different fields, including medical services and industry.

2. Delicate Advanced mechanics: Nature's Adaptability and Flexibility

Delicate mechanical technology, propelled by the adaptability and flexibility of organic entities like octopuses, has arisen as a field looking to make robots with additional regular developments. These robots, frequently produced using delicate and adaptable materials, track down applications in operations, search and salvage missions, and conditions where customary unbending robots might battle to explore.

VI. Correspondence Innovations: Nature's Language Decoded

1. Bio-Propelled Signal Handling
   The investigation of creature correspondence, from the unpredictable moves of bumble bees to the sonar route of bats, has motivated advancements in signal handling. By getting it and imitating the productivity of organic correspondence frameworks, engineers have created advancements for worked on remote correspondence, detecting, and route.

2. Swarm Knowledge in Systems administration

Swarm knowledge, saw in friendly bugs, has roused the advancement of calculations for effective systems administration and data handling. By emulating the decentralized and cooperative dynamic cycles found in nature, these calculations add to the advancement of correspondence organizations and the Web of Things (IoT).

VII. Clinical Progressions: Nature's Recuperating Insight

1. Biomimetic Medication Conveyance Frameworks
   The circulatory arrangement of the human body has enlivened the plan of biomimetic drug conveyance frameworks. These frameworks, displayed after the proficiency of blood dissemination, mean to work on the designated conveyance of drugs inside the body. The standards of biomimicry in drug conveyance upgrade remedial adequacy while limiting secondary effects.

2. Bio-Enlivened Imaging Advances

Mechanical headways in clinical imaging draw motivation from nature's mind boggling detecting components. Advancements like manufactured opening radar, motivated by bat echolocation, add to further developed imaging goal and analytic abilities. By copying nature's detecting modalities, these advances improve clinical diagnostics and treatment arranging.

VIII. Challenges and Moral Contemplations

1. Moral Components of Biomimicry
   While biomimicry holds extraordinary commitment for mechanical advancement, it additionally raises moral contemplations. The apportionment of natural plans and cycles for human use might have unseen side-effects, both for environments and the species being imitated. Finding some kind of harmony between mechanical headway and moral obligation is pivotal in the utilization of biomimetic standards.

2. Biodiversity Preservation and Mindful Advancement

As biomimicry picks up speed, there is a developing consciousness of the need to focus on biodiversity preservation. Capable advancement includes guaranteeing that biomimetic applications don't add to the abuse or danger of normal species. Moral biomimicry thinks about the possible effects on biological systems and pursues feasible and amicable concurrence among innovation and nature.

7.1 Bio-inspired Robotics and Engineering

The universe of mechanical technology and designing has gone through an extraordinary development with the rise of bio-enlivened plan standards. Drawing motivation from the intricacies of the normal world, researchers and architects have wandered into the domain of bio-propelled mechanical technology, trying to imitate and upgrade the unimaginable capacities saw in living creatures. This investigation digs into the entrancing space of bio-motivated mechanical technology and designing, disentangling the manners by which nature's diagram has turned into a directing power for development in the production of robots and high level designing frameworks.

1. Underpinnings of Bio-roused Mechanical technology: Mirroring Nature's Creativity
1. Biomimicry as a Plan Worldview
   Biomimicry, the act of imitating nature's plans and cycles, fills in as the essential worldview for bio-roused advanced mechanics. By concentrating on the mind boggling systems and versatile procedures found in natural living beings, engineers gain experiences into effective answers for complex designing difficulties.
   This approach has prompted the advancement of robots that not just copy the structure and capability of their natural partners yet additionally outperform them in specific viewpoints.
2. Developmental Calculations: Nature-Roused Issue Solvers

Developmental calculations, roused by the standards of regular choice and hereditary advancement, have become useful assets in bio-motivated mechanical technology. These calculations reenact the course of advancement to enhance the plan and usefulness of mechanical frameworks. Through iterative patterns of determination and change, architects can show up at arrangements that copy the productivity and versatility saw in natural development.

II. Movement Motivated Essentially's Ability

1. Legged Movement: Imitating the Collective of animals
   The variety of legged movement in the animals of the world collectively has propelled the improvement of legged robots that can explore testing landscapes with deftness and versatility. From bug motivated hexapods to quadrupedal robots suggestive of vertebrates, bio-propelled legged velocity is upsetting fields like pursuit and salvage, investigation, and military applications.

2. Serpentine Mechanical technology: Drawing from Snakes and Worms

Serpentine robots, enlivened by the crawling movement of snakes and worms, offer extraordinary benefits in exploring bound spaces and harsh territories. Impersonating the undulating developments of these animals, serpentine robots have applications in examination undertakings, operations, and calamity reaction situations where customary wheeled or legged robots might battle to move.

III. Delicate Advanced mechanics: Bridling Nature's Adaptability

1. Delicate bodied Organic entities as Motivations
   Delicate advanced mechanics, portrayed by the utilization of agreeable materials and adaptable designs, draws motivation from delicate bodied life forms tracked down in nature. From the fragile developments of octopuses to the pliability of worms, delicate mechanical technology duplicates nature's adaptability. Delicate robots succeed in situations that request communication with fragile conditions, like in clinical applications or human-robot coordinated effort.

2. Octopus-Roused Arms: Controlling with Effortlessness

The able and adaptable arms of octopuses have propelled the advancement of delicate automated controllers. Emulating the construction and developments of octopus arms, these bio-roused controllers exhibit prevalent versatility and control capacities. Applications range from submerged investigation to fragile surgeries where accuracy is fundamental.

IV. Aeronautical Advanced mechanics: Taking Off with Avian Motivation

1. Bird-Roused Flight Elements
   The dominance of flight displayed by birds has been a directing power in the improvement of elevated mechanical technology. From the fluttering wings of hummingbirds to the taking off trip of hawks, engineers try to reproduce avian flight elements. Bio-enlivened elevated robots, or ornithopters, influence wing morphologies and wing-beat designs saw in birds for upgraded mobility and effectiveness.

2. Bat Flight: Spry and Proficient in the Air

Bats, with their extraordinary wing construction and flight designs, have enlivened progressions in ethereal advanced mechanics. Bat-motivated drones, known as "bat-bots," integrate adaptable wing structures and refined echolocation frameworks for route. These bio-roused airborne robots succeed in mind boggling and jumbled conditions, exhibiting the versatility of nature's plans.

V. Swarm Advanced mechanics: Cooperative Ways of behaving Motivated by Bugs

1. Subterranean insect Motivated Coordination
   Swarm advanced mechanics, drawing motivation from the aggregate ways of behaving of social bugs like insects, accentuates decentralized and cooperative ways to deal with critical thinking. Subterranean insect motivated calculations guide the coordination and correspondence among enormous gatherings of robots. Swarm advanced mechanics finds applications in undertakings like investigation, reconnaissance, and natural checking.
2. Honey bee Enlivened Route

The many-sided route capacities of honey bees, depending on decentralized independent direction and correspondence through dance, have propelled swarm mechanical frameworks for investigation and planning. By emulating the productive and decentralized nature of honey bee settlements, engineers expect to make independent automated swarms fit for organizing complex undertakings in unstructured conditions.

VI. Detecting and Insight: Copying Nature's Sensors

1. Bio-Motivated Vision Frameworks
   Nature's visual frameworks, from according to bugs to according to hunters like birds, move headways in mechanical vision. Bio-enlivened vision frameworks influence standards like all encompassing perspectives, movement discovery, and profundity insight for improved automated discernment. Applications incorporate independent vehicles, observation, and mechanical examination assignments.
2. Echolocation: Duplicating Bat-Propelled Sonar

Bat-enlivened sonar frameworks, known as bio-sonar, have affected the improvement of mechanical detecting advances. By imitating the echolocation capacities of bats, these frameworks empower robots to explore and see their environmental factors in conditions where customary sensors might be deficient. Applications range from advanced mechanics in dim conditions to submerged investigation.

VII. Human-Machine Points of interaction: Spanning the Organic and the Counterfeit

1. Cerebrum PC Points of interaction: Connecting Brain and Machine
   Bio-propelled designing stretches out to human-machine interfaces, with mind PC interfaces (BCIs) trying to lay out direct correspondence between the human cerebrum and machines. Drawing motivation from brain processes, BCIs mean to unravel mind cues for controlling mechanical appendages, prosthetics, and, surprisingly, outer gadgets, opening additional opportunities for assistive advances and neuroprosthetics.
2. Biomimetic Prosthetics: Incorporating with the Human Body

Prosthetic appendages planned with biomimetic standards intend to repeat the regular developments and elements of natural appendages. By contemplating the biomechanics of human development, engineers make prosthetics that answer brain signals, giving clients a more instinctive and normal experience. Biomimetic prosthetics add to the rebuilding of versatility and usefulness for people with appendage misfortune.

VIII. Difficulties and Future Headings

1. Mechanical Difficulties in Biomimetic Plan
   Regardless of the wonderful advancement in bio-enlivened mechanical technology and designing, challenges continue. Repeating the complexities of regular frameworks frequently requires conquering innovative obstacles connected with material science, energy proficiency, and the combination of complex tactile and activation frameworks. Headways here will assume a urgent part in understanding the maximum capacity of bio-motivated plans.
2. Moral Contemplations in Bio-propelled Advanced mechanics

As bio-motivated mechanical technology keeps on progressing, moral contemplations come to the front line. Questions encompassing the moral utilization of bio-mimicry, possible ecological effects, and the limits of coordinating living life forms with machines raise significant moral quandaries. Dependable advancement in bio-propelled mechanical technology requires cautious thought of these moral aspects.

7.2 Applications of Vertebrate Locomotion Research

The investigation of vertebrate movement, with its rich embroidered artwork of developmental variations and biomechanical complexities, has not just extended how we might interpret the regular world yet has additionally prepared for imaginative applications across different fields. From mechanical technology and prosthetics to sports science and restoration, the bits of knowledge acquired from vertebrate movement research have turned into an impetus for headways that span the domains of science and innovation.

1. Bio-roused Advanced mechanics: Exploring New Wildernesses
   One of the most noticeable utilizations of vertebrate motion research is in the domain of bio-enlivened mechanical technology. By analyzing and understanding the standards basic the assorted methods of vertebrate development, engineers have created robots that copy the proficiency and versatility saw in nature. For example, robots enlivened by the legged headway of creatures like cheetahs and bugs feature improved readiness and mobility, making them appropriate for search and salvage missions, investigation in testing landscapes, and, surprisingly, military applications.
   Moreover, the investigation of fish impetus components has affected the plan of submerged robots that mirror the undulating developments of fish tails. These bio-propelled submerged vehicles succeed in undertakings like sea investigation, natural observing, and submerged prehistoric studies. By utilizing the standards of vertebrate velocity, bio-enlivened mechanical technology opens new boondocks in independent frameworks fit for exploring complex conditions with a degree of readiness and productivity beforehand unequaled.
2. Prosthetics and Restoration: Reestablishing Portability with Biomimicry
   Vertebrate movement research has essentially added to the advancement of biomimetic prosthetics, planning to reestablish portability and usefulness for people with appendage misfortune. By contemplating the biomechanics of normal appendage developments in vertebrates, scientists plan prosthetic appendages that intently mirror the regular scope of movement and flexibility.
   For instance, understanding the mechanics of human stride has prompted the making of prosthetic appendages outfitted with cutting edge joint frameworks and tactile criticism systems. These headways upgrade client solace, versatility, and by and large personal satisfaction for handicapped people. The incorporation of vertebrate movement standards into prosthetic plan mirrors an agreeable mix of science and designing, offering people with appendage misfortune the chance to recapture a more regular and natural walk.
   In restoration, bits of knowledge from vertebrate motion research

are applied to the advancement of assistive gadgets that guide in reestablishing versatility for people with development issues or wounds. Mechanical exoskeletons, enlivened by the biomechanics of human and vertebrate appendages, offer help and help with restoration works out. By fitting these gadgets to copy normal development designs, restoration endeavors become more designated and successful, working with quicker recuperation for patients.

3. Sports Science and Execution Improvement: Acquiring the Upper hand

The investigation of vertebrate headway has significant ramifications in the domain of sports science, where understanding the biomechanics of development can prompt execution improvement and injury avoidance. Competitors and mentors attract on this information to streamline preparing regimens, further develop strategies, and plan gear that lines up with the standards of proficient motion. For instance, experiences from the running biomechanics of cheetahs have impacted the plan of particular athletic footwear. Runners benefit from shoes intended to imitate the usefulness of a cheetah's paw, enhancing foothold and security. Additionally, the investigation of avian flight has roused progressions in streamlined features, affecting the plan of athletic gear like bikes, caps, and bathing suits.

In sports medication, the standards of vertebrate motion add to injury counteraction systems and restoration programs. Understanding the biomechanics of joints and muscles helps tailor preparing schedules to upgrade strength, adaptability, and in general athletic execution while limiting the gamble of wounds.

4. Ergonomics and Human-Machine Collaboration: Planning for Effectiveness

The use of vertebrate motion research stretches out to ergonomics and human-machine connection, where the objective is to configuration instruments and points of interaction that adjust flawlessly with human development designs. By concentrating on the normal ergonomics of vertebrate appendages and joints, planners make gadgets that improve client solace, lessen weakness, and upgrade productivity.

In the plan of connection points for PCs, cell phones, and other advanced gadgets, the standards of vertebrate motion guide the arrangement and usefulness of controls.

This guarantees that clients can collaborate with innovation such that mirrors normal developments, decreasing the gamble of monotonous strain wounds and upgrading by and large convenience.

5. Figuring out Neurological Issues: Bits of knowledge for Medical care

The investigation of vertebrate headway gives important experiences into the working of the sensory system and the components hidden development control. This information is essential in the field of medical services, especially in understanding and treating neurological problems that influence versatility.

Examination into the brain circuits and control systems engaged with vertebrate movement adds to progressions in neurorehabilitation and the advancement of mediations for conditions like spinal line wounds, Parkinson's illness, and stroke. By unwinding the complexities of how the cerebrum facilitates development, researchers can devise designated treatments and recovery procedures to work on engine capability and upgrade the personal satisfaction for people with neurological problems.

7.3 Potential for Future Innovations

As we stand at the slope of another time, set apart by fast headways in innovation, science, and interconnected worldwide difficulties, the potential for future advancements is both extensive and extraordinary. From the combination of man-made consciousness and biotechnology to forward leaps in practical energy and space investigation, the scene of potential outcomes is huge. This investigation digs into the potential for future developments across disciplines, imagining a reality where human inventiveness and mechanical headways impel us into unfamiliar domains.

1. Union of Man-made reasoning and Biotechnology: The Ascent of Bioinformatics
1. Accuracy Medication and Customized Medicines
   The crossing point of man-made reasoning (artificial intelligence) and biotechnology holds the commitment of reforming medical services through the rise of bioinformatics. High level calculations and AI models, fit for handling immense measures of genomic information, will empower the ID of customized treatment plans custom-made to a person's hereditary cosmetics. This shift towards accuracy medication can possibly change the adequacy of clinical mediations, improving results and limiting incidental effects.
2. Simulated intelligence Improved Medication Revelation

The regular medication revelation process is in many cases tedious and asset serious. The mix of man-made intelligence into drug revelation speeds up this cycle by foreseeing potential medication competitors, streamlining sub-atomic designs, and recognizing promising targets.

This intermingling takes into consideration more proficient ID of novel treatments, prompting the quick improvement of medicines for infections that were once viewed as impressive difficulties.

II. Quantum Figuring: Rethinking the Limits of Calculation

1. Dramatic Computational Power

The coming of quantum registering addresses a change in perspective in the realm of data handling. Quantum PCs influence the standards of quantum mechanics to perform estimations at speeds out of reach by old style PCs. This dramatic expansion in computational power has extraordinary ramifications for fields like cryptography, enhancement issues, and complex reenactments. Quantum PCs can possibly unwind secrets in material science, recreate atomic designs for drug disclosure, and alter information encryption.

2. Quantum Computerized reasoning

The collaboration between quantum processing and man-made consciousness frames the establishment for quantum computerized reasoning (QAI). QAI outfits the equal handling capacities of quantum PCs to upgrade AI calculations. This combination of advances could prompt forward leaps in design acknowledgment, improvement, and information examination, opening new boondocks in man-made intelligence applications and speeding up development in different ventures.

III. Economical Energy Arrangements: Towards a Green Unrest

1. High level Energy Stockpiling Innovations

The mission for supportable energy arrangements is a squeezing worldwide test, and what's to come holds promising developments in cutting edge energy capacity innovations. From cutting edge batteries with higher energy densities to novel materials for capacitors and supercapacitors, headways in energy capacity are vital for the boundless reception of environmentally friendly power sources. These developments will assume a vital part in tending to discontinuity issues related with environmentally friendly power, making ready for a more solid and economical energy lattice.

2. Fake Photosynthesis for Carbon Impartial Powers

Roused ordinarily's course of photosynthesis, specialists are investigating counterfeit photosynthesis as a way to deliver carbon-unbiased fills. Using particular impetuses and sustainable power sources, fake photosynthesis expects to catch and change over carbon dioxide into significant energizes. This development holds the possibility to upset the energy scene by giving a feasible and versatile answer for moderate fossil fuel byproducts and fulfill the developing need for clean energy.

IV. Space Investigation and Colonization: Past Earth's Viewpoint

1. Lunar and Martian Territories

   The investigation and possible colonization of divine bodies, including the Moon and Mars, address a boondocks for future developments. Headways in advanced mechanics, 3D printing, and life emotionally supportive networks will be instrumental in laying out feasible territories past Earth. These developments might make ready for human settlements on different planets, introducing another period of interplanetary investigation and extending the limits of human civilization.

2. Space-Based Sun oriented Power

Space-based sun oriented power (SBSP) includes catching sun powered energy in space and sending it remotely to Earth. This creative way to deal with energy age could address the limits of earthbound sun oriented power, like evening time and environmental obstruction. With headways in space transportation and sunlight based power catch innovations, SBSP holds the possibility to give a consistent and plentiful wellspring of clean energy, adding to worldwide supportability endeavors.

V. Neurotechnology and Cerebrum PC Points of interaction: Opening the Psyche's True capacity

1. Improved Mental Capacities

   The area of neurotechnology is ready to open the maximum capacity of the human mind, prompting advancements that upgrade mental capacities. Cerebrum PC interfaces (BCIs) may empower direct correspondence between the mind and outer gadgets, opening opportunities for consistent data trade, upgraded memory, and expanded learning. These progressions could upset instruction, correspondence, and human-PC associations.

2. Brain Inserts for Neurological Issues

Brain inserts and neurostimulation innovations hold guarantee for treating neurological problems by tweaking the movement of brain circuits. Advancements in scaled down, biocompatible gadgets could give designated mediations to conditions like Parkinson's sickness, epilepsy, and discouragement. These neurotechnological progressions might offer customized and exact arrangements, working on the personal satisfaction for people impacted by neurological issues.

VI. Moral and Administrative Contemplations: Exploring the Future Capably

1. Moral Systems for artificial intelligence and Biotechnology
   As advancements unfurl, moral contemplations become foremost. Laying out vigorous moral systems and guidelines is fundamental to guarantee capable turn of events and sending of advancements, especially in the domains of man-made intelligence and biotechnology. Resolving issues connected with protection, predisposition in calculations, and the capable utilization of hereditary data is essential for encouraging confidence in arising advances and defending against unseen side-effects.
2. Worldwide Coordinated effort and Administration

The potential for future advancements rises above public boundaries, requiring worldwide cooperation and administration components. Multilateral endeavors to address moral, legitimate, and cultural ramifications of arising advances will be urgent in cultivating a worldwide local area that explores the difficulties and advantages of development on the whole. Cooperative drives can work with the sharing of information, assets, and best works on, adding to an additional comprehensive and impartial future.

Chapter 8

Conservation Implications

Even with heightening biodiversity misfortune, living space debasement, and the approaching danger of environmental change, preservation endeavors have become basic to protect the planet's biological equilibrium. This investigation digs into the complex ramifications of protection, looking at the difficulties, techniques, and the groundbreaking effect of preservation drives on environments, species, and human social orders. As we explore a time set apart by ecological vulnerability, understanding the preservation suggestions becomes principal in manufacturing an economical future.

1. Biodiversity Misfortune: The Desperation of Preservation Activity
1. Biological system Strength and Versatility
   Biodiversity fills in as the groundwork of biological system strength and versatility. Different biological systems show more noteworthy flexibility to ecological changes, guaranteeing their capacity to endure unsettling influences like environment variances, sickness flare-ups, and intrusive species. Protection endeavors assume a urgent part in safeguarding biodiversity, in this way reinforcing the strength of environments and their ability to give fundamental biological system administrations.
2. Compromised and Jeopardized Species

The downfall of species around the world, many drove to the edge of annihilation, highlights the earnestness of preservation. Whether because of territory misfortune, poaching, contamination, or environmental change, the deficiency of species upsets natural equilibrium and lessens the planet's organic lavishness. Preservation drives intend to safeguard and restore jeopardized species, alleviating the unfavorable impacts of anthropogenic exercises and advancing the recuperation of biological systems.

II. Territory Safeguarding and Rebuilding: Supporting Environment Wellbeing

1. Safeguarded Regions and Biodiversity Areas of interest
   Laying out safeguarded regions and saving biodiversity areas of interest are significant methodologies in the preservation toolbox. These assigned regions act as asylums for a huge number of animal groups, giving places of refuge where verdure can flourish undisturbed. The conservation of biodiversity areas of interest, portrayed by high species endemism, guarantees the assurance of exceptional and indispensable parts of the worldwide biota.
2. Biological Reclamation and Rewilding

Past safeguarding, protection endeavors progressively center around biological reclamation and rewilding. Reclamation includes restoring corrupted biological systems, switching living space discontinuity, and once again introducing local species. Rewilding, a more aggressive methodology, looks to reestablish normal cycles and once again introduce cornerstone species, cultivating the recovery of whole biological systems. These intercessions plan to restore natural equilibrium and work on the general strength of environments.

III. Environmental Change and Protection Difficulties

1. Changed Environments and Reach Movements
   Environmental change presents imposing difficulties to preservation by modifying territories and setting off shifts in species' reaches. As temperatures increase, numerous species face the test of adjusting to changing climatic circumstances or moving to additional reasonable environments. Preservation endeavors should represent these movements, including the production of environment strong halls, helped relocation methodologies, and versatile administration practices to shield species confronting territory changes.
2. Protection in a Warming World

The heightening effects of environmental change request imaginative preservation techniques. This incorporates creating environment brilliant protection plans, integrating environment demonstrating into dynamic cycles, and carrying out measures to alleviate and adjust to the evolving environment. Protectionists should expect the intricate interaction between environmental change and biodiversity misfortune, making progress toward arrangements that address both prompt dangers and long haul supportability.

IV. Human-Natural life Struggle: Adjusting Protection and Livelihoods

1. Rivalry for Assets

   Preservation endeavors frequently converge with human exercises, prompting clashes over assets. As human populaces extend and infringe upon normal environments, rivalry for assets like land, water, and food escalates. This opposition can bring about clashes among untamed life and networks, with ramifications for both biodiversity protection and human vocations.

2. Moderating Struggles and Advancing Conjunction

Moderating human-untamed life struggle requires a fragile harmony between preservation objectives and the necessities of nearby networks.

Procedures might include executing non-deadly hindrances, getting domesticated animals fenced in areas, and creating maintainable business choices for networks dwelling in nearness to untamed life territories. Compelling protection perceives the significance of neighborhood commitment, encouraging conjunction among people and natural life.

V. Protection and Native Information: Collaborations for Feasible Practices

1. Customary Natural Information

   Native people group frequently have rich customary natural information (TEK) aggregated over ages. This information envelops experiences into neighborhood environments, supportable asset the board rehearses, and the unpredictable connections among people and nature. Perceiving and integrating TEK into protection procedures can improve the adequacy of drives by adjusting them to the nuanced comprehension of biological systems held by native networks.

2. Local area Based Protection Approaches

Local area based protection, grounded in the standards of coordinated effort and shared administration, incorporates neighborhood networks into dynamic cycles. By engaging networks to play a functioning job in preservation, these methodologies cultivate a feeling of pride and stewardship over normal assets. This upgrades the progress of protection drives as well as adds to the safeguarding of social variety and conventional practices.

VI. Protection and Practical Turn of events: A Nexus for Progress

1. Biological system Administrations and Human Prosperity
   Protection is complicatedly connected to human prosperity through the arrangement of biological system administrations. Biological systems convey crucial administrations like clean water, fertilization of yields, and environment guideline. Perceiving the interconnectedness of environments and human social orders highlights the significance of preservation in supporting the underpinnings of life and supporting practical advancement objectives.
2. Maintainable Asset The board

Preservation systems lining up with economical asset the board are basic for guaranteeing the life span of environments and the networks dependent on them. Adjusting the extraction of assets with recovery processes, carrying out quantities for fishing and logging, and taking on supportable rural practices are vital parts of preservation endeavors that add to the prosperity of the two environments and human populaces.

VII. Protection Innovation and Advancement: Instruments for Compelling Preservation

1. Remote Detecting and Observing
   Headways in remote detecting advances, including satellite symbolism and automated airborne vehicles (UAVs), have altered protection checking. These devices empower researchers to evaluate changes in land cover, track natural life populaces, and screen deforestation in close to constant. Remote detecting upgrades the proficiency and extent of protection endeavors, giving significant information to confirm based direction.
2. Resident Science and Publicly supporting

Drawing in general society in protection through resident science and publicly supporting drives enhances the range and effect of preservation projects. Volunteers contribute information on untamed life sightings, natural surroundings conditions, and obtrusive species through advanced stages. This cooperative methodology improves information assortment as well as encourages a feeling of aggregate liability regarding biodiversity protection.

VIII. Protection Morals and Backing: Molding Public Discernment

1. **Moral Contemplations in Preservation**
   The moral elements of protection stretch out to inquiries of equity, value, and the inherent worth of biodiversity. Preservation drives should explore moral contemplations connected with migration of networks, the treatment of hostage creatures, and the prioritization of specific species over others. Moral structures guide dynamic cycles to guarantee that protection activities line up with standards of reasonableness, straightforwardness, and regard for every living being.
2. **Public Mindfulness and Backing**

Molding public insight and gathering support for protection objectives require successful correspondence and backing. Protection associations and researchers assume a critical part in dispersing data, bringing issues to light about biodiversity misfortune, and motivating activity. Public help converts into political will, subsidizing potential open doors, and a more extensive cultural obligation to manageable practices.

8.1 Human Impact on Vertebrate Locomotion

The many-sided dance of vertebrate movement, finely tuned by a long period of time of development, faces exceptional difficulties directly following human exercises. The effect of human presence on the assorted exhibit of vertebrate species, from land to air and ocean, resounds through biological systems around the world.

This investigation dives into the complex manners by which human exercises impact vertebrate headway, inspecting the biological strings that wind through earthly, elevated, and amphibian conditions.

1. **Land-Based Motion: The Changed Ways of Earthbound Species**
1. **Living space Discontinuity and Interruption**
   Human-actuated changes to scenes, including urbanization, horticulture, and framework advancement, have prompted boundless territory discontinuity. For earthly vertebrates, for example, warm blooded creatures and reptiles, this fracture disturbs conventional movement courses, searching examples, and favorable places. As normal territories become separated pockets encircled by human-ruled scenes, species face difficulties in exploring modified landscapes and experiencing novel deterrents.
2. **Street Mortality and Obstructions**

The multiplication of streets represents a huge danger to earthbound vertebrates. Expanded vehicular traffic brings about street mortality, influencing species going from little warm blooded creatures to huge vertebrates like deer and bears. Streets additionally go about as hindrances, obstructing the development of creatures and adding to populace disconnection. Procedures, for example, untamed life halls and passages expect to relieve these effects by giving safe entries to creatures to cross human-ruled scenes.

II. Elevated Headway: Skies Modified by Human Designs

1. Crashes with Structures and Correspondence Pinnacles
   Birds, the bosses of the sky, face difficulties acted by human designs such like tall structures and correspondence towers. Crashes with these designs, frequently connected with intelligent surfaces, bring about fatalities for various bird species. The nighttime route of relocating birds is especially helpless to disturbances brought about by enlightened structures. Preservation measures, including bird-accommodating structure plans and lighting guidelines, intend to lessen the effect of human designs on avian movement.

2. Environmental Change and Adjusted Movement Examples

Environmental change acquaints a powerful aspect with the elevated movement of birds. Modified temperature designs, changes in wind flows, and moving accessibility of assets impact the timing and courses of avian movement. Species that depend on exact timing for relocation and reproducing may confront difficulties in synchronizing their developments with changing natural signals. Understanding and moderating the effects of environmental change on avian movement designs are basic for the protection of transitory bird species.

III. Sea-going Motion: Exploring Human-Altered Streams

1. Dam Development and Riverine Biological systems
   The development of dams has significant ramifications for sea-going vertebrates, especially fish. Dams adjust riverine environments, hindering the regular progression of waterways and upsetting fish movement. Many fish species, known for their exceptional swimming capacities, face obstructions in their upstream developments for generating. Fish stepping stools and other fish section arrangements endeavor to alleviate these effects, empowering fish to explore past dams.

2. Overfishing and Marine Relocations

In marine conditions, overfishing has repercussions on the velocity of fish species participated in significant distance movements. Over-exploitation disturbs regular populace elements, influencing the overflow and circulation of transient species. For marine creatures like whales and ocean turtles, human exercises, for example, delivery and water-front advancement present dangers to their transient courses. Preservation endeavors center around laying out marine safeguarded regions and manageable fishing practices to protect the complicated relocations of marine vertebrates.

IV. Human-Prompted Transformative Tensions: Adjusting to Anthropogenic Changes

1. Fast Advancement In light of Human Exercises
   Human exercises apply particular tensions on vertebrate populaces, driving quick developmental changes. Models incorporate metropolitan dwelling species advancing attributes that improve endurance in metropolitan conditions, like changed conduct and physiology. Now and again, creatures adjust to human-prompted changes in their current circumstance, showing attributes that guide in exploring scenes overwhelmed by human exercises. Understanding these developmental reactions is fundamental for anticipating the drawn out effects of human-prompted changes on vertebrate velocity.
2. Transformative Compromises and Protection Suggestions

While quick advancement can give benefits in adjusting to human-modified conditions, it frequently includes compromises. Transformations that improve endurance in metropolitan scenes might come at the expense of diminished execution in regular living spaces. Protectionists wrestle with the test of saving normal ways of behaving and biological jobs while perceiving the developmental changes driven by human exercises. Adjusting the preservation of species' inherent qualities with their ability to adjust is a complex and developing errand.

V. Contamination and Foreign substances: Disabled Motion Across Conditions

1. Water Contamination and Sea-going Portability
   Sea-going conditions endure the worst part of contamination, affecting the motion of fish and other amphibian vertebrates. Synthetic poisons, plastics, and supplement spillover add to water debasement, influencing the swimming capacities of fish. In outrageous cases, contamination can prompt physiological irregularities and impeded

swimming execution. Preservation endeavors center around relieving contamination through wastewater the executives, territory reclamation, and public mindfulness crusades.

2. **Air and Commotion Contamination: Influencing Avian Way of behaving**

Air and commotion contamination change the acoustic and environmental scenes in which birds explore. Birds depend on vocalizations for correspondence, domain foundation, and route. Clamor contamination from human exercises, like traffic and modern tasks, disrupts these correspondence signals. Moreover, impurities in the air might affect respiratory capability in birds, impacting their perseverance and generally speaking abilities to fly. Understanding and moderating the impacts of air and commotion contamination are fundamental for protecting avian motion.

VI. Obtrusive Species and Changed Collaborations: Molding Environmental Elements

1. Predation Tensions and Conduct Movements
   The presentation of obtrusive species disturbs laid out biological elements, impacting the velocity of local vertebrates. Obtrusive hunters can apply new predation pressures on local species, changing their way of behaving and development designs. For example, flightless birds on islands might confront expanded weakness to presented hunters. Preservation methodologies include the evacuation or control of obtrusive species to reestablish natural equilibrium and relieve the effects on local vertebrate movement.
2. Rivalry for Assets and Specialty Relocation

Obtrusive species frequently contend with local species for assets, prompting specialty relocation. This opposition can impact the dispersion and development examples of local vertebrates. Earthbound warm blooded animals, for instance, may encounter changes in searching way of behaving and spatial use because of rivalry with presented species. Preservation endeavors incorporate methodologies to oversee and control intrusive species, permitting local vertebrates to keep up with their regular headway designs.

VII. Amusement and The travel industry: Exploring the Effect on Untamed life

1. Unsettling influence and Social Changes
   The prospering the travel industry and sporting exercises carry

people into nearness with untamed life territories. This expanded human presence can upset normal ways of behaving and headway examples of vertebrates. Species might modify their development because of unsettling influences, influencing taking care of, reproducing, and relocation. Preservation systems include capable the travel industry rehearses, environment drafting, and government funded instruction to limit the effect of sporting exercises on natural life velocity.

2. Ecotourism and Protection Potential open doors

While sporting exercises present difficulties, very much oversaw ecotourism can introduce open doors for protection. Income created from capable ecotourism drives can subsidize preservation endeavors and living space assurance. Finding some kind of harmony between giving chances to individuals to encounter untamed life and limiting unsettling influence to vertebrate velocity requires cautious preparation and adherence to moral and feasible ecotourism rehearses.

VIII. Protection Morals and Human Obligations: Fashioning an Agreeable Future

1. Moral Contemplations in Preservation
   The effect of human exercises on vertebrate motion raises moral contemplations that reach out past natural elements. Protection endeavors should wrestle with inquiries of moral treatment of untamed life, the freedoms of individual creatures, and the obligations of people in forming the conditions they share with vertebrates. Moral systems guide dynamic cycles to guarantee that protection activities focus on the government assistance of both human and non-human partners.
2. Schooling and Backing for Concurrence

Training assumes a critical part in cultivating a feeling of obligation and understanding among people in general. Protection associations and specialists participate in backing endeavors to bring issues to light about the effect of human exercises on vertebrate headway. Advancing conjunction includes cultivating an association among individuals and the regular world, underlining the significance of regarding the environmental necessities of vertebrates while addressing human requirements for improvement and progress.

8.2Conservation Challenges for Species with Unique Locomotor Adaptations

In the tremendous embroidered artwork of biodiversity, certain species stand apart for their phenomenal locomotor variations. These transformations, finely tuned by development, empower these animals to explore assorted conditions, from the skies to the profundities of the sea. Notwithstanding, these very transformations that characterize their uniqueness likewise render them defenseless against a heap of protection challenges. This investigation dives into the complicated snare of difficulties confronting species with unmistakable locomotor transformations, unwinding the intricacies of their protection despite ecological changes, territory misfortune, and human effects.

1. Arboreal Wonders: Difficulties for Species in Overhang Domains
1. Deforestation and Fracture
   Arboreal species, adjusted for life in the treetops, face serious dangers from deforestation and territory fracture. As immense stretches of woodlands are cleared for farming, logging, and urbanization, the complicated covering territories significant for species like primates, sloths, and different birds are divided. This upsets their capacity to navigate the backwoods shade proficiently, influencing taking care of, rearing, and social communications. Protection endeavors should address the underlying drivers of deforestation and advance the safeguarding of coterminous shade environments.
2. Network and Passage Difficulties

Keeping up with network between timberland pieces is fundamental for arboreal species with tremendous home reaches. Disturbed network presents difficulties for their versatility, hereditary variety, and long haul endurance. Preservation systems include the making of shade spans, untamed life hallways, and safeguarded pathways that empower arboreal species to move unreservedly through the treetops. Guaranteeing these species can cross their natural surroundings is fundamental for keeping up with sound populaces and saving the biological jobs they play in woodland environments.

II. Airborne Marvels: Protection Ups and Downs for Avian Ability

1. Movement Dangers and Changing Flyways
   Birds that set out on exceptional transitory excursions face various dangers along their flyways. Human-prompted changes in scenes, environment, and food accessibility influence the timing and progress of movements. For species like Icy terns and bar-followed godwits, adjustments in conventional visit destinations and disturbances in

the accessibility of assets present preservation challenges. Securing and reestablishing key living spaces along transient courses and tending to environment related shifts are essential for the preservation of these avian miracles.

2. Impacts and Urbanization

The skies, once sweeping and unhampered, are progressively loaded up with human designs that posture gambles for aeronautical species. Crashes with structures, correspondence pinnacles, and wind turbines compromise the existences of birds in flight. Urbanization further mixtures these difficulties, changing the scene and presenting dangers like light contamination. Protection measures include planning bird-accommodating designs, directing metropolitan turn of events, and carrying out relief systems to decrease the effect of human designs on avian headway.

III. Amphibian Wonders: Exploring Pained Waters

1. Dams and Obstruction Impacts
    Amphibian species, going from fish to marine vertebrates, face difficulties acted by human framework such like dams. Dams upset regular riverine environments, blocking the transitory pathways of fish and changing the progression of water. For species like salmon, known for their wonderful capacity to explore upstream for generating, dam developments present huge preservation challenges. Fish stepping stools and other fish section arrangements intend to moderate these impacts, permitting sea-going species to keep up with their regular movement designs.
2. Plastic Contamination and Marine Relocations

Marine species with many-sided locomotor transformations, including whales, dolphins, and ocean turtles, experience dangers from plastic contamination in seas. The ingestion of plastic, ensnarement in trash, and contamination related medical problems influence their capacity to explore immense marine movements. Preservation endeavors center around lessening plastic contamination, executing mindful waste administration rehearses, and laying out marine safeguarded regions to protect the transient courses and natural surroundings of these oceanic wonders.

IV. Cursorial Heroes: Protection Steps for Earthly Speedsters

1. Territory Misfortune and Fracture
    Earthbound speedsters, adjusted for quick stumbling into scenes, face protection challenges emerging from living space misfortune

and discontinuity. The change of regular environments into agrarian land, metropolitan regions, and framework hallways upsets the huge scopes expected by species like cheetahs and pronghorns. Divided natural surroundings impede their capacity to participate in high velocity pursuits, affecting hunting, mating, and generally speaking environmental jobs. Protection methodologies include saving enormous, interconnected living spaces and making halls to work with the development of these cursorial bosses.

2. Environmental Change and Moving Regions

The effect of environmental change presents an extra layer of intricacy for cursorial species. Changes in temperature, precipitation examples, and vegetation influence the accessibility of assets and impact the dispersion of prey species. Variation to changing ecological circumstances requires the capacity to navigate new regions, presenting difficulties for species with particular locomotor transformations. Protection endeavors should address the interconnected difficulties of territory safeguarding, environment flexibility, and keeping up with the natural equilibrium of earthly biological systems.

V. Merged Development and Preservation Intersection

1. Exceptional Difficulties of Joined Advancement
Species that have advanced concurrently, creating comparative locomotor transformations regardless of particular developmental narratives, face novel protection challenges. Models incorporate the united advancement of smoothed out body structures in dolphins and ichthyosaurs for proficient oceanic movement. Protection methodologies need to think about the particular transformations of joined species, recognizing their common weaknesses and the requirement for fitted ways to deal with address the dangers they face.

2. Preservation Cooperative energies and Shared Arrangements

Focalized development likewise opens roads for protection collaborations. Species with comparative locomotor transformations might profit from shared protection methodologies. For instance, preservation measures pointed toward safeguarding amphibian natural surroundings benefit the two dolphins and manatees. Perceiving these common arrangements permits protectionists to use shared characteristics in locomotor transformations to address the difficulties looked by focalized species all the more really.

VI. Human-Untamed life Struggle and Preservation Morals

1. Struggle Over Space and Assets
   As human populaces grow and infringe upon regular living spaces, clashes among people and untamed life raise. Species with one of a kind locomotor transformations might confront expanded rivalry for space and assets, prompting human-natural life clashes. Tending to these struggles requires a nuanced comprehension of the biological necessities of these species and carrying out methodologies that advance concurrence while defending human interests.
2. Moral Contemplations in Protection Practices

Monitoring species with novel locomotor transformations requests moral contemplations in protection rehearses. Movements, hostage rearing, and different intercessions should focus on the government assistance and normal ways of behaving of the species in question. Protection morals assume a crucial part in directing dynamic cycles, guaranteeing that the safeguarding of phenomenal locomotor transformations lines up with standards of regard, sympathy, and natural trustworthiness.

VII. Protection Innovation: Instruments for Saving Novel Locomotor Variations

1. Following and Observing Advances
   Headways in following and observing advances give priceless experiences into the developments and ways of behaving of species with novel locomotor transformations. GPS collars, satellite labels, and bioacoustic observing empower analysts to accumulate information on the going examples, relocation courses, and vocalizations of these species. This data is pivotal for planning powerful protection systems that address the particular locomotor necessities of every species.
2. Protection Robots and Elevated Studies

Protection drones outfitted with cameras and sensors offer a non-nosy method for reviewing enormous regions and observing natural life. Airborne overviews give information on territory use, populace densities, and the effect of human exercises on scenes. For species with novel locomotor transformations, these advances help in recognizing key natural surroundings, movement courses, and likely dangers, illuminating designated preservation mediations.

VIII. Public Mindfulness and Promotion: Connecting with for Preservation Achievement

1. Training and Effort Drives
   Public mindfulness and commitment are urgent for the progress of preservation endeavors focusing on species with novel locomotor transformations. Instructive drives, outreach projects, and local area contribution bring issues to light about the biological significance of these species and the preservation challenges they face. Building public help cultivates a feeling of aggregate liability regarding the safeguarding of these remarkable creatures and their multifaceted locomotor transformations.
2. Promotion for Preservation Arrangements

Promotion assumes a critical part in molding preservation strategies that address the particular requirements of species with remarkable locomotor variations.

Preservation associations and concerned people can advocate for the foundation of safeguarded regions, the authorization of untamed life assurance regulations, and the execution of supportable land-use rehearses. Viable backing guarantees that protection arrangements are educated by logical information and focus on the safeguarding of the locomotor transformations that characterize these species.

8.3 Preserving Biodiversity in the Face of Habitat Change

Biodiversity, the multifaceted snare of life enveloping different species, is confronting uncommon difficulties following natural surroundings change. As human exercises change scenes, modify environments, and add to environmental change, protecting biodiversity turns into a squeezing basic. This investigation digs into the intricacies of preserving biodiversity in the midst of living space change, looking at the diverse difficulties and the procedures fundamental for keeping up with the rich embroidered artwork of life on The planet.

1. Natural surroundings Change: A Moving Scene for Biodiversity
1. Anthropogenic Effect on Natural surroundings
   Human exercises, going from urbanization and horticulture to deforestation and foundation improvement, have prompted significant changes in normal territories. These modifications upset the sensitive equilibrium of biological systems, influencing the accessibility of assets, favorable places, and movement courses for various species. The speed and size of anthropogenic natural surroundings change present difficulties for biodiversity, as species should adjust to new circumstances or face the gamble of populace decline and termination.

2. Environmental Change and Territory Disturbance

Environmental change compounds territory change by adjusting temperature and precipitation designs, affecting the dissemination of species and the organization of biological systems. The moving environment might deliver existing natural surroundings unsatisfactory for specific species, constraining them to relocate, adjust, or face decline. Polar bears, for instance, are significantly impacted as softening ocean ice decreases their hunting grounds. Tending to the effects of environment prompted natural surroundings change is vital for defending biodiversity in a warming world.

II. Preservation Difficulties In the midst of Environment Change

1. Living space Fracture and Disengagement
   Living space change frequently prompts fracture, breaking persistent scenes into disengaged patches. This fracture presents difficulties for species that depend on broad territories for taking care of, rearing, and relocation.
   Disconnected populaces face hereditary bottlenecks, decreased admittance to mates, and expanded weakness to ecological aggravations. Preservation endeavors should address natural surroundings network through the making of untamed life passageways and safeguarded regions to moderate the adverse consequences of discontinuity.
2. Intrusive Species and Changed Environment Elements

As environments change, intrusive species might take advantage of new biological specialties, outcompeting or going after local species. This modifies the elements of environments, influencing biodiversity at different trophic levels. Protection procedures include observing and overseeing intrusive species, reestablishing local territories, and carrying out measures to forestall the presentation and spread of obtrusive life forms.

III. Versatile Methodologies for Biodiversity Preservation

1. Natural surroundings Reclamation and Restoration
   Notwithstanding living space change, dynamic reclamation and recovery endeavors become pivotal for keeping up with biodiversity. Living space reclamation includes returning corrupted regions to a more regular state, while recovery centers around working on the biological elements of changed territories. Establishing local vegetation,

reestablishing wetlands, and executing maintainable land-use rehearses are fundamental parts of these versatile techniques.

2. Environment Tough Preservation Arranging

Protection arranging should integrate environment flexibility to guarantee the drawn out feasibility of biodiversity. This includes recognizing regions that are probably going to stay stable or become reasonable under future environment situations. Making safeguarded regions and untamed life saves in these versatile zones gives shelters to species to endure the difficulties presented by environment prompted territory change.

IV. Network Preservation: Connecting the Holes

1. Natural life Hallways and Green Foundation
   Network protection centers around keeping up with or reestablishing the availability of natural surroundings, permitting species to move uninhibitedly across scenes. Untamed life halls, green belts, and natural organizations act as pathways that empower the development of species, working with quality stream, movement, and variation. Integrating these highlights into metropolitan preparation and foundation improvement is critical for safeguarding biodiversity even with living space change.

2. Movement and Helped Relocation

In circumstances where species face quick dangers because of living space misfortune, movement and helped relocation might be thought of. These mediations include migrating people or populaces to regions with additional appropriate circumstances. While disputable and requiring cautious thought of moral, natural, and hereditary elements, movement can give a help to animal groups in danger of elimination because of quick territory change.

V. Public Mindfulness and Promotion: Encouraging Preservation Responsibility

1. Natural Instruction and Effort
   Raising public mindfulness about the significance of biodiversity and the effects of environment change is a foundation of successful preservation. Natural schooling programs, outreach drives, and local area commitment endeavors add to building a protection ethic. Educated and connected with networks are bound to help strategies and practices that focus on biodiversity preservation despite territory change.

2. Backing for Supportable Practices

Backing assumes an essential part in advancing economical practices that moderate territory change and its effects on biodiversity. People, people group, and associations can advocate for approaches that focus on preservation, supportable land-use arranging, and capable asset the executives. By encouraging an aggregate obligation to biodiversity protection, backing adds to forming a more practical connection between human exercises and the normal world.

www.ingramcontent.com/pod-product-compliance
Lightning Source LLC
LaVergne TN
LVHW010341200726
843507LV00010B/1601